IMAGES
of America

FRANKFORT

IMAGES
of America

FRANKFORT

Rachel Gilmore with the
Frankfort Area Historical Society

ARCADIA
PUBLISHING

Published by Arcadia Publishing
Charleston, South Carolina

Library of Congress Control Number: 2012942345

For all general information, please contact Arcadia Publishing:
Telephone 843-853-2070
Fax 843-853-0044
E-mail sales@arcadiapublishing.com
For customer service and orders:
Toll-Free 1-888-313-2665

Visit us on the Internet at www.arcadiapublishing.com

*This one is for Dan and the Frankfort Preservation Foundation,
who got me thinking about the value of honoring the past in
public ways, and for all of the Burts, Frans, Henrys, Franks,
Dorothys, Roberts, Richards, Erises, Happys, and Pauls who
lived Frankfort and loved Frankfort and who I feel I now know.
From generation to generation, this one is for all of you.*

CONTENTS

ACKNOWLEDGMENTS

I would like to thank Judy Herder and the Frankfort Area Historical Society board for partnering with me on this project, Judy Schultz for her assistance tracking down details, and all of the current and former members of the society who wrote and researched, preserved and prepared documents that I used while researching Frankfort histories. I apologize for any omissions or errors. They were not intentional.

Unless otherwise noted, all photographs are courtesy of the Frankfort Area Historical Society archives and used with the society's permission.

INTRODUCTION

Frankfort is known as the village with 1890s charm, and its people and places have tightly woven that vintage thread of community spirit across generations for over 150 years.

Initial settlers in the area came from New England along the old Sauk Trail and were hearty pioneers willing to brave an unpopulated prairie, or, rather, a prairie populated by Native Americans. In the 1830s, L.M. Clayes established a homestead and the first post office in an area named Chelsea, about a mile west of Frankfort. When the Black Hawk War came to Illinois, many early pioneer families retreated from the danger, and Chelsea was completely abandoned in 1848. By the mid-1850s, however, when the Joliet and Northern Indiana Railroad came through Frankfort township, families with the names Haass, Clayes, McDonald, Doty, Stephen, Cleveland, Carpenter, and Letts had begun to put down permanent roots. Soon, German and Swiss immigrant families followed, like the Kohlhagens, Baumgartners, Scheers, Eisenbrandts, Heusners, Mingers, Lambrechts, Knaters, Breiderts, Baumanns, Folkers, and others.

In 1879, the residents of Frankfort voted to incorporate, calling their village Frankfort Station, after the township, which was named by Frederick Cappel, who came to the area from Frankfurt am Main, Germany. Cappel's new homeland was located on the highest spot between Chicago and the Mississippi River, with clean water, rolling prairie, wooded groves, and fertile farmland providing a wealth of possibilities for early residents. With such opportunity and natural resources, Frankfort (*Station* was eventually dropped) quickly grew into its role of little village on the prairie, serving as a local center for transportation and commerce, as well as social, educational, religious, and cultural activities, building community spirit all the while.

By the turn of the century, Frankfort had two railroad lines running through town. It boasted several taverns, a post office, a community band hall, two bands, a livery, a hotel, several general stores, a two-story department store, a furniture maker, an undertaker, a two-story school, a town doctor, wagon makers, farm implement dealers, a hardware store, a creamery, two active churches, multiple civic organizations, a telephone line (in 1901), and a sense of community that rivaled the most established East Coast towns. By the end of the first decade, the trolley would arrive, further connecting residents to the outside world and making a high school education more accessible. When Lincoln Highway (also known as Route 30) rolled through in 1920, Frankfort was really on the map, literally and figuratively.

During the 1950s, however, when Frankfort's rapid growth was leveling off, residents looked back at their little town and took stock of where they were and where they wanted to go. They staged a five-day centennial celebration, honoring Frankfort's first 100 years: 1890s costumes were required, vintage activities entertained attendees, a ball was held, and a state senator came to speak. Best of all, the financial focus of the event was to raise money for a community park, something the residents agreed was necessary for the welfare of the village. The town raised almost $7,800 and paid off the mortgage on the park property previously purchased. Shortly after this, in 1959, the chamber of commerce formed, and area merchants and village officials agreed that capitalizing on the village's historic architecture and inherent charm would benefit the community in many ways. So began a community focus on preservation with a purpose.

Looking back through the early records of Frankfort, seeing the faces in the photographs of those who have gone before, and reading the writings of those who lived in and loved their hometown, it is clear that Frankfort continually fosters a sense of unity and identity perhaps common to small towns but uncommon in its longevity. Decade after decade, from generation to generation, old-fashioned American values continue to shape Frankfort, without limiting its ability to adapt to changing times. From historic preservation to memorials of important people, to civic, religious, recreational, and educational organizations, to village officials who plan for the future while respecting the past, residents continue to be engaged in their town, as they have for over 150 years.

While the years have not always been idyllic, and economic downturns have affected the village like they have other communities, Frankfort's down-home community spirit continues to provide a firm foundation from which to regroup and rebound. From the ongoing rebirth of the historic downtown business district to the evolution of Sauerkraut Days into the nationally ranked Frankfort Fall Festival, to the rails-to-trails conversion of the Michigan Central Railroad tracks, to the preservation of Frankfort's iconic landmarks the Grainery and the water tower, Frankfort values its heritage while clearly envisioning its future.

In 2006, Dan Hattan, founder and first president of the Frankfort Preservation Foundation, a grassroots organization founded in 1993 and dedicated to preserving the past for the sake of the future, wrote these words about the water tower:

> The historic water tower, when it first faced the wrecking ball in 1993, has come to symbolize, for many, the important role it has in shaping the connection between the past, present and future of Frankfort. It stands as gatekeeper and guardian of the spirit of our Frankfort founders and the vigilant oversight of today's citizenry. It looms from our historic center to gaze upon our ever-expanding neighborhoods. It connects us all to each other and our past.

From generation to generation, Frankfort has journeyed from little town on the prairie to thriving small suburb of Chicago, never straying too far from home.

One

FROM GENERATION
TO GENERATION

No matter people are in Frankfort, they can likely hear or see something that reminds them of the founding families. Street names recall those who created Frankfort: Bowen Street for Sherman W. Bowen, who platted the village; Carpenter Street for N.A. Carpenter, who owned the first general store; McDonald Lane for John McDonald, who was the first village president; Elsner Road for the Elsner family, who farmed land just west of downtown for over 100 years. Kohlhagen Park was dedicated to honor the Kohlhagen families, active in business and village government. Breidert Green pays tribute to Burt Breidert, a successful businessman, village administrator, and founder of the chamber of commerce. Frankfort is filled with the spirit of those who lived here decades ago, working, raising families, sharing in the joys and sorrows of neighbors and friends, and supporting the community, whether through attending band concerts, donating to youth athletic teams, or volunteering at Frankfort Fall Festival, which draws a few hundred thousand people to town each Labor Day weekend.

In a Frankfort Area Historical Society 1993 newsletter, Henry Heusner, who grew up in Frankfort in the 1930s, recalls this about the people of his past: "As Frank [Folkers] said, so many of us left that sleepy little town to seek our 'fortunes' elsewhere and seldom returned. One thing we could not leave behind, however, were the values we learned from the role models and heroes we worshipped as children. I can recall most vividly so many of mine. The passing years seem to bring out deeper meanings."

From generation to generation, Frankfort is a village that connects itself, neighbor to neighbor, and weaves a thread of community spirit through fabric life.

Charles C. Holden
CHICAGO
FORMERLY OF FRANKFORT TP.

The Honorable Charles C.P. Holden was one of Frankfort's first residents, arriving in 1836 at the age of nine with his family, who made a claim of 160 acres at Skunk Grove on the headwaters of Hickory Creek in Frankfort. According to lifelong former resident Harlan Eisenbrandt, that area was located about a half mile north of Route 30 and a half mile east of Route 45.

Early resident John Baumgartner of Switzerland actually made five trips across the Atlantic Ocean before settling permanently in Frankfort along Hickory Creek. On one of his trips, he brought six siblings back to America with him. One brother, Jacob, settled in Frankfort and opened the cheese factory known as the Hickory Creek Creamery. Another brother, Benedict, owned a general store in town. On John's fifth and final Atlantic crossing, he brought his bride, Maria (Mary), whom he married in 1853. John and Maria Baumgartner are pictured here.

Caspar Eisenbrandt came to Frankfort with his family from Germany. The 1860 census lists him as a laborer at age 20 (approximately the same time as this photograph). A family history notes that Caspar married Dorthea Yost, who owned a home at 139 White Street in Frankfort. She also supported the family, as Caspar was said to prefer not to work regularly. The couple had 11 children and still has descendants living in Frankfort.

Orrin B. Cleveland is pictured here with his trotter in Frankfort in 1870. Orrin was the elder brother of William, and according to census records of the time, lived with William on his large farm northwest of the village along Route 30. This labeled photograph was discovered in a Braceville, Illinois, antique shop by Frankfort resident and historical society member John Herder.

John and Maria Kohlhagen were married in 1870 and bought the 160-acre farm (now Cardinal Lake subdivision) from John's father Fritz for $8,000 in 1875. In the 1890s, the couple (left) moved into the village where John opened a general store with his son Frank. The Kohlhagen farm eventually sold to Swift & Company, which used it as a research farm until it was sold and subdivided for homes. On October 19, 2003, the Frankfort Park District dedicated Kohlhagen Park at 108th Avenue and Cardinal Lake Drive (below) with Kohlhagen descendants in attendance.

August and Freida Werner were married in Green Garden Township just south of Frankfort on September 24, 1874. One year earlier, Werner had opened his wagon shop, which later became a farm implement and sewing machine business. The couple had one daughter, Ida, and lived on Ash Street just south of Nebraska Street in a home between the shop and the warehouse.

Johnson Folkers came to America from Germany with his uncle in 1849. He worked as a farmhand and, later, a teamster until purchasing land in Frankfort in 1863. He then opened Frankfort's first meat market and eventually bought out the livery and finally the old Doty hotel, turning these businesses over to his sons in 1889. Pictured here are Johnson's grandchildren in 1893 with their ponies. From left to right are Glenn, Leo, Florence, Lucille, Clarence, and Herbert P. Folkers. Johnson's son, Frank, stands in the doorway.

Frank and Emma Kohlhagen married in 1896, and, for many years, Frank ran the general store with his father, John, on the southeast corner of Oak and Kansas Streets. This store had been in existence since 1855, started by N.A. Carpenter and later operated by Benedict Baumgartner in the same location. Frank was a pillar of the community, serving as a village clerk and trustee, as well as a director on the organizing board of the Frankfort State Bank.

John and Margaret (Leppla) Staff were married in 1891 in Frankfort by Reverend Lambrecht at St. Peter's Evangelical and Reformed Church. A newspaper write-up of their 50th anniversary mentions that "Jesus Leads" was the theme of their wedding, a song performed again during their anniversary service. John Staff was a lifelong railroad man, working primarily for the Elgin, Joliet & Eastern Railway. The couple is pictured here in their yard at Carpenter and Bowen Streets, probably in the 1920s.

A group of Frankfort's first businessmen and community leaders are shown gathered at the Michigan Central Railroad depot, likely in the 1890s. Pictured from left to right are Fred Leppla (one-term village clerk), August Baumann (village trustee), "Jumbo" Charles Haass, John Bobzin (village trustee), unidentified, and August Wischover (village trustee).

For over 100 years, the Elsner family farmed a large parcel of land on what was then the west edge of town where Joliet Street (paralleled Michigan Central tracks, now gone) met Elsner Road. Descendant Dorothy Elsner Porter still lives in Frankfort today. Pictured here in front of the farmhouse in the early 1900s, from left to right, (first row) are Dorothy's grandparents Caroline (Koppelman) and Charles Elsner and her great-grandmother Sophia Wrede Elsner; (second row) her father George Elsner (back left) and her uncle Henry Elsner (back right).

By the late 1880s, cigar smoking had become widely popular in the United States, with Illinois boasting over 1,100 cigar factories in 1885. (A resident of Frankfort was even rumored to have a home-based rolling business.) And, although it was considered improper for ladies to smoke, this 1926 postcard shows the Minger and Hansen women smoking at a family reunion on the Minger farm south of Frankfort. Pictured, from left to right, are (front) toddler Bettie Tewes Lane and two unidentified children; (middle) unidentified, Oledine Woelfel, Emma Minger Luhring, Lena Minger Woelfel, and Julia Minger Buck; (rear) George Buck.

Dr. Emil Haass, a former Civil War surgeon, wore many hats in Frankfort. He served eight years as village president and six as trustee in the late 1800s, as well as being the town doctor. His office and house were located at what is now 213 Kansas Street, and he was reported to have a well-stocked library and a love for storytelling.

Doctor Haass also had a lifelong interest in photography, and he annually organized a New Year's photograph to show the past and present year at the stroke of midnight. Pictured here from left to right are (first row, floor) unidentified and George Haass; (second row, seated) Lena Bankow, Dr. Emil Haass, Alice Haass Zahn, Emma Haass Cadden, ? Bauch with dog; (third row, standing) unidentified, "Jumbo" Charles Haass, Irene Haass, unidentified, Max Haass, and Frank Bauch.

Bernard Balchowsky came to Frankfort as a peddler who sold goods from a pack on his back. From there, he branched out to a horse and wagon, finally opening up a department store at the southeast corner of Ash and Kansas Streets in 1877. In 1910, Balchowsky looked back on his 33 years in business, saying: "I feel thankful and proud of the fact that I have always kept every promise I made, and never caused any worry to those who first helped me get my start."

17

Emma Klepper, daughter of Minnie and Henry Klepper, worked at B. Balchowsky & Sons beginning in 1906. According to a 1910 store brochure, Emma always "followed our advice and policy of treating all customers alike, so that now the customers can only think of calling her Emma, and not Miss Klepper, as some would be called."

Members of the Folkers family pose in their Brush auto. The vehicle was one of the first cars available to middle- and working-class individuals and was designed to handle bumpy or muddy country roads, making it popular with farmers and other rural residents. It featured a hardwood chassis, axles, and wheels, as well as shock absorbers and coil springs. Pictured are (front) "Grandpa" Henry Folkers; (back, from left to right) Tillie Folkers, Henry Folkers, and Dick Folkers.

18

The Sippels were another founding family of Frankfort. Father Conrad owned several businesses in town over the years, including a farm implement shop on the corner of Nebraska and Oak Streets and a saloon down the block at Kansas and Oak Streets. The saloon later became an ice cream parlor, candy store, and newsstand, eventually run by daughter Amelia/Katie (right) and her husband, Christ Fink. At one point, sister Margaret (left) also worked in the confectionery, while sister Emma (center) taught piano.

Dorothy Elsner Porter and her husband, Robert, moved back to Frankfort in 1951 from the St. Louis area. Robert was a photographer (many of his photographs are featured in this book), as well as a police officer and a member of Frankfort's civil defense. The couple was active at St. Peter's Church and other community events. Dorothy continues to help the Frankfort Area Historical Society with background research on life in the 1900s in Frankfort. (Courtesy of the Robert Porter Collection.)

Paul Lambrecht, son of an insurance broker, was born and raised in Frankfort. Pictured here in 1937 with his dog, Paul went on to enlist in the Army and later work for his father's insurance agency. After marrying Vicki Gerodimos in 1947, Paul and a friend, "Bitz" Brown, borrowed $3,500 each and started Brown & Lambrecht Earthmovers, which grew into a successful grading and construction company with projects across the United States.

Dr. Walter Hedges arrived in Frankfort in 1908 after finishing medical school and soon took over Dr. Hamlin's practice. His office was connected to his home at 34 Nebraska Street, and he was known for treating patients whether or not they could pay. Dr. Hedges also started a full service medical clinic in 1950. His wife, Irma, was very dedicated to the community, as well, volunteering in the school and through Women's Club. The couple is pictured here during a trip to Hawaii. (Courtesy of the Hedges Collection.)

Viola Lankenau, pictured here in 1955, grew up in Frankfort and became the intermediate teacher at Frankfort Grade School, teaching third, fourth, and fifth grades. Later, she became the principal of Frankfort Grade School and served the district for 42 years total. Students remember her for being firm but fair. Each spring, a scholarship in her honor is offered to one graduating eighth grader by the District 157-C parent–teacher organization. (Courtesy of the Robert Porter Collection.)

Eris Rudman (right) is pictured here with friends and fellow residents Tillie Wischover (left) and Maridell Condon. Eris was a tireless champion of Frankfort, helping purchase land for Main Park before there even was a park district and later driving friends and neighbors to the polls to vote "Yes" for the referendum to create the new taxing body. Although the first attempt failed, the park district issue passed in 1968, realizing Eris's dream.

According to fifth-generation Frankfort resident Chip Krusemark, Nanny the sheep lived with five other sheep, two horses, one rabbit, one dog, one cat, and one pet raccoon named Leroy on his family's property on Sauk Trail just east of downtown. While the big yellow house is still there, the barn burned down in 1978. Both Chip's father and grandfather were local attorneys, land developers, and philanthropists. (Courtesy of Chip Krusemark.)

Upon moving to Frankfort in 1967, Maggi Lindee joined the Women's Club while husband, Carl, joined the historical society. The couple went on to champion preservation and community-building efforts in their new hometown together, as Maggi later joined and ran the Frankfort Area Historical Society. "It's better to be involved. It's soul satisfying," Maggi was once quoted as saying. Maggi is pictured here as the female half of the couple from Grant Wood's *American Gothic* at a downtown Frankfort event in the early 1980s. With her is Norman Jansky.

Former Frankfort mayor Glenn Warning stands next to his bust, placed in a small rose garden outside the Glenn R. Warning Building at 123 Kansas Street (now home to the Frankfort Chamber of Commerce). A Frankfort businessman, Glenn served as a village trustee for six years and mayor for over 30, as well as in other elected positions outside the village. His family owned and still operates a bus company, originally the Gold Star Line and now Warning Charter. (Photograph by Rachel Gilmore.)

Dan Hattan, far right, stands with his fellow park district board running mates. From left to right are Paul Shaffer, Dean Vaundry, and Phil Simmons, pictured after a hotly contested 2005 election in which Dan organized the Frankfort First Coalition to endorse candidates with similar goals. Hattan was also president of the Frankfort Preservation Foundation at the time and a founding member of that grassroots preservation group.

Retired US Congressman George E. Sangmeister (pictured center) was born in Frankfort to Rose and George C. Sangmeister, who served as mayor for 32 years. A Democrat from a Republican-leaning community, George E. nonetheless followed in his father's footsteps and earned a stellar reputation for putting his constituents first and working for the greater good, regardless of party politics. The Abraham Lincoln National Cemetery in Joliet came into being largely due to the congressman's unwavering commitment to honor those who served America. Pictured here shortly before his death in 2007, Congressman Sangmeister admires the busts dedicated in his and his father's honor with his wife, Doris (left), and son, Kurt (right). The Frankfort Preservation Foundation commissioned the busts and placed them in the Preservation Park Sculpture Garden on the grounds of the Founders Center at 140 Oak Street in Frankfort. (Photograph by Rachel Gilmore.)

Two

A Firm Foundation

Frankfort's historic architecture is one of its most appealing features. Stepping out on the downtown sidewalks, it is easy to imagine what life might have been like here 100 years ago, as many of the same buildings remain, restored and repurposed for life in the 21st century. One of the original general stores is still a general store, filled with all things quaint, charming, and nostalgic. Houses surrounding the downtown area range from American Farmhouse to Queen Anne to Craftsman to Prairie, many lovingly restored by residents who are reclaiming the home's history for their own.

Burt Breidert, lifelong Frankfort resident until his retirement and Frankfort's first village administrator, wrote the poem "Hometown," about the value of preservation. The following excerpt reveals Frankfort's long-term commitment to preservation with a purpose:

The new who come to open shop / Or join our present bounds, / Must meet our codes, preserve the past, / Or quickly leave our grounds. / This shall require the will and strength / From boards, who recognize / Some growth may bring us more concerns, / Which then increase with size. / So growth that meets our well-planned ways, / Which blends with treasured past, / Will minimize the impact on / The life-style we have cast. / Our future lies with what we do / And what is done with care. / The quality of life right here / Is judged by years of wear.

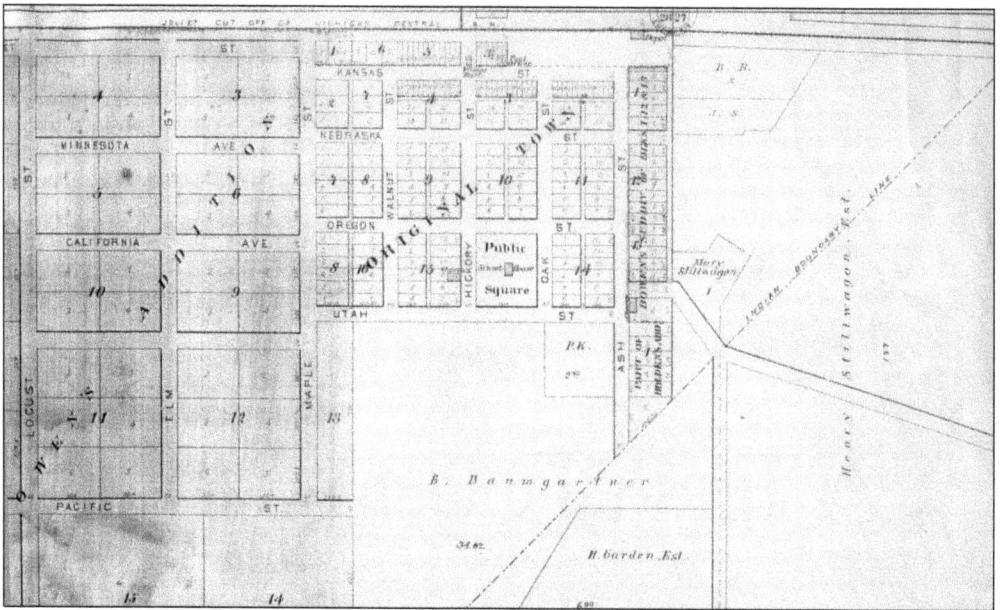

As one of the oldest plats of Frankfort, this 1873 drawing shows the layout of the residential area in Frankfort, as mapped out by Sherman W. Bowen. Bowen worked for the Joliet and Northern Indiana Railroad in Joliet but wisely bought 80 acres surrounding the depot in Frankfort. The village hall at Kansas and Hickory Streets (now the Frankfort Chamber of Commerce building), the post office (now Old Plank Trail Tavern), the depot (a rebuilt depot now stands there), and the public square with schoolhouse (now the site of the park district's main offices and program space) are all clearly marked.

This drawing from the 1873 plat book shows the business and residence of one of the founding fathers, Thomas Herschbach. The home and hardware store were built in 1867 on the south side of Kansas Street just west of Oak Street. In 1882, the house was moved to its present location at 120 Oak Street. The site of the hardware store is now owned by G.T. Luscombe and once housed the fire department. St. Peter's original wood frame church can be seen in the background.

James Letts was a grain dealer in Frankfort, settling here in 1855. He later went into partnership with a man named Williams to operate the old Doud Hotel at the corner of Kansas and Hickory Streets. This 1873 plat book drawing shows the hotel and livery across the street, which were later bought by Johnson Folkers.

The Cleveland farm straddled Route 30 just west of Wolf Road. This 1873 plat book drawing looks south over Route 30. The Dinkey can be seen at the top of the photograph, making its return trip to Joliet on the Michigan Central tracks. Cleveland was one of the original settlers in Frankfort township in 1844 and later served as postmaster for seven years. His farm encompassed a heavily wooded area along the banks of Hickory Creek about a mile north and two miles west of Frankfort's downtown.

This home was owned by Ebenezer Stephen, another founding father of Frankfort. It sat west of the end of Elwood Street and just north of the railroad tracks, which appear to run along the bottom of this photograph. Ebenezer owned a carriage, wagon, and farm implement shop with his brother David at the corner of Smith and Elwood Streets. His son Robert later became a postmaster in town for 20 years.

A Baptist church was built at the corner of Nebraska and Hickory Streets in 1863 with David Letts as the first pastor. The building was later moved to the rear of the property and became the garage of the beautiful Queen Anne (pictured here) that sits on the lot. St. Peter's Evangelical and Reformed Church also worshipped here in the garage structure until their own wood frame church was built at the corner of Sauk Trail and Ash Street in 1868.

RES OF LEVI DOTY ESQ THANKFORT WILL CO ILL

Levi Doty, whose father, Ambrose, settled in the area in 1834, owned a large tract of land in town from which he bought and sold horses. This stately home (above) on Nebraska Street still stands, although the large stable seen at the rear of the property was split in two and converted to two individual homes that face Oregon Street to the south. The garage of the main home was built with wood from the Pony Express relay station located along the small creek at the western edge of the property. In addition to his horse-trading, Levi Doty was also a humane officer and operated the Humane Home for Horses (below), caring for animals whose owners no longer could. Levi kept a water trough filled at the edge of the street so that travelers could water their faithful friends along the way. "Be merciful to your horses," reads the inscription in the stone trough wall, still embedded in the property on Nebraska Street.

ESTABLISHED IN 1880
LIFE IS TOO SHORT TO BE SPENT IN UNNECESSARY SUFFERING.
IF I CAN DO ANYTHING FOR YOU, LET ME DO IT NOW.

SNOWFLAKE IN 1882.   SNOWFLAKE IN 1902.

Sold to A. H. Shreffler, of Joliet, in 1883, and after doing his Master faithful service, returned to his Old Home in August, 1902, to spend the balance of his days. Snowflake was foaled in March, 1875, and was with us until 1906.
I am always ready to attend to cases of cruelty.
NO CHARGE FOR HUMANE SERVICES
INTERSTATE PHONE 61

LEVI DOTY
FRANKFORT, WILL COUNTY, ILL.   HUMANE HOME FOR HORSES.
NEVER PROSECUTE UNLESS ABSOLUTELY NECESSARY.

Frankfort's first schoolhouse was a one-room log cabin. Residents, however, valued education and raised the $5,000 needed to build this modern, two-story frame structure in 1870. By the 1920s, the building was no longer up to code, according to school officials. Current resident Dorothy Porter remembers the wooden schoolhouse being moved to the edge of the curb on Oak Street while construction of a modern brick structure took place behind it.

Conrad Sippel stands outside his saloon at the southwest corner of Oak and Kansas Streets in the late 1800s. Note the new-looking wooden sidewalks in the foreground. After Frankfort incorporated in 1879, the village board made an ordinance that business owners provide and maintain a sidewalk at least three feet wide. The hitching fence posts in front were the result of another ordinance after officials got tired of replacing broken lampposts pulled down by horses.

Old Creamery & Bridge.
Frankfort, Ill.

This postcard of the Hickory Creek Creamery (above) represents an early thriving industry in Frankfort that operated from 1875 to 1895. Owner Jacob Baumgartner and brother John produced cheese and butter, which they then shipped out to Chicago and other towns via area railroad lines. Hickory Creek ran along the south edge of the property, and ice cut from the creek during the winter months provided year-round refrigeration. Sadly, after production stopped, the creamery sat abandoned for almost 100 years. When road construction on Route 45 forced the relocation of the building to a site on Route 30 east of Route 45 (below), area residents had great hopes for a renovation/restoration project. However, the historic structure fell into greater disrepair and was demolished in 2011 because of public safety concerns.

In 1855, the Joliet & Northern Indiana Railroad tracks were laid in Frankfort, providing a "milk and mail" run for those living along the line. When the Michigan Central Railroad bought the line in the 1870s, its little twice-a-day passenger train affectionately became known as "The Dinkey." A poem written by W.G. Struthers in 1894 commemorating this Frankfort favorite begins this way: "There's a small country village not far from here / A village that's been there for many a year. / And though honored by time it ne'er has grown greater / Than two stores, a Post Office and a grain elevator. / And four times a day there's The Dinkey." Much like the rather short-lived trolley line that passed through Frankfort, The Dinkey's usefulness as a passenger train decreased with the rise of the automobile in the 1920s.

The first water tower in Frankfort was built of wood and metal in 1894. The tank, tower, all 3,620 feet of pipe, and 11 fire hydrants gave Frankfort residents their first modern water system. This structure survived the Folkers Livery fire across the street in 1910 but was decommissioned in 1915, when a new 100,000-gallon all-metal tower was built at the same location. When village officials decided to stop using that tower altogether in 1993 and prepared to dismantle it, a grassroots organization called the Frankfort Preservation Foundation emerged and raised the funds needed to save the village landmark. The group continues to dedicate itself to saving and preserving other pieces of Frankfort's history.

This aerial photograph of Kansas and Ash Streets was likely taken from the granary tower just before the turn of the century, as there are no telephone wires or trolley tracks visible. The white house owned by Orville Pyle that stood in the middle of Kansas Street next to B. Balchowsky & Sons is seen in the lower left of the photograph, while Zechlin's Furniture is the two-story white building on the opposite (south) end of that block. Baumann's Tavern is the long, light-colored building on the corner.

Frank Kohlhagen (front right) stands with several of his employees in the grocery store he and his father, John, owned. At one point, John lived in the large and stately home south of the grocery store at Oak and Nebraska Streets, which featured a quarry stone foundation to facilitate the cold storage of produce and other items sold in the store. Also pictured are, from left to right, Elsa Lankenau, Ricka Harnack, and unidentified.

Pleasant Hill Cemetery on Elsner Road was a natural final resting place for early settlers, as the ground was high and even, with many mature trees. The oldest headstone is dated 1845. In 1875, the Frankfort Cemetery Association held its first meeting, elected a board, and established rules of use, pictured above. In 1894, the association changed the name to Pleasant Hill Cemetery. In the photograph below (likely from the turn of the century), a funeral procession wends its way west out of town on Kansas, making a right turn onto Maple Street. It would have then turned left on Joliet Street, crossed the Michigan Central tracks in front of the Folkers icehouse (north of the current Frankfort fire station), and followed Joliet Street west to the entrance of the cemetery. In 1884, the association voted to assess each lot owner $1 to build a fence across the front of the cemetery, as constant horse and foot traffic on Joliet Street, which eventually connected with Route 30 northwest of town, led to much damage of the grounds.

Originally built by H.P. Bock in 1856 at 112 Kansas Street, this building first served as a harness shop. As years passed, and automobiles replaced horses and the need for harnesses, resident George Haass bought the building and opened a barbershop. Dirty towels and other laundry from the business were taken by train (and later, trolley) to Joliet to be cleaned and returned. In 1910, the shop was open seven days a week, in part to accommodate farmers in town for Sunday church, and offered haircuts for 15¢ and shaves for 10¢.

Built in 1889, the Elgin, Joliet & Eastern Railway passed through the south end of Frankfort. The depot for this busy freight route sat just west of Center Road on the north side of the tracks. As track use had declined over the years, Canadian National Railway's 2007 proposal to buy the line and increase traffic caused much controversy among village residents. However, the deal closed in early 2009, and the route is again in regular use.

Henry Eisenbrandt's American Farmhouse–style home stood at 20 North Smith Street, and he worked a few doors south as a blacksmith on the current Fra-Milco Cabinet Company property. Henry's family is pictured here: from left to right, Amelia (back) and children Arthur, Mabel, and Frank. Henry was the son of Caspar Eisenbrandt.

This postcard shows Hickory Street looking north from Nebraska Street. An unidentified boy rides his bike, while an unidentified girl and woman stand to the left. The house behind them stood in what is now the parking lot for LaSalle St. Securities. Clues help date the photograph to the first decade of the 20th century. Note the telephone poles on the right (phone service came to the village in 1901) and the old wooden Folkers Livery peeking through the trees on the left (burned in 1910).

An example of American Farmhouse architecture common to Frankfort in its early days, the Conrad and Emma Wilson house on Smith Street reflects simplicity and function. The kitchen tended to be oversized to accommodate large families, farmhands, or food production (canning, pickling, baking, preserving, and so forth). As families expanded, the homes often took on a sprawling look as bedrooms were added or even a second floor. The parlor, however, was small and reserved for special occasions.

This large building on Kansas Street in between Ash and Oak Streets was the residence and business of John Bruggeman, who operated Bruggeman's Buffet. This 1909 photograph shows John's ever-expanding family in front of the restaurant. From left to right are (first row) LeRoy, Donald, and unidentified; (second row) Charlotte, John, Wilhelmena, Anna, and Esther. An unidentified man stands to the left of the family.

Ash St. looking North, Frankfort, Ill.

42205.

The Schoenherr blacksmith shop was one of four smithies in Frankfort. It sat on the northwest corner of Oregon and Ash Streets, near the Klepper wagon shop and Bettenhausen and Knater harness shop. A Frankfort Grade School newsletter from October 28, 1938, notes that the children were excited when the old blacksmith shop was torn down: "We, the children of the school, think it will make a great improvement to the town." The shop dated back to the Civil War era.

This 1910 photograph, taken from the second floor of the Folkers Hotel, looks northeast over Kansas Street. The grain elevator built by D.W. Hunter in 1894 is on the left. To the right, note the wide limestone sidewalk. The man facing the camera is about to walk up a few steps past the barbershop and the barber pole at the street edge under the balcony. The decorative stone columns of the old Citizen's Bank are visible to the right of the barber's balcony.

Pictured above, B. Balchowsky & Sons, at the corner of Ash and Kansas Streets, served Frankfort as a full-service, two-story department store. A 1910 store brochure states that two clerks handled each department in order to make sure that customers could always find exactly what they needed. It also reminded patrons that, "One price has always been our rule." From its start as a general store in 1877, the business eventually carried not only groceries and dry goods but also hardware, furniture, appliances (such as they were), and clothing. The photograph below shows the Stoves and Crockery Department on the second floor. In addition, shoppers could find rugs, carpets, linoleums, and oilcloths. "Only the best is what we offer—a policy we carry throughout the store," reads the 1910 brochure.

This postcard shows the first St. Peter's Evangelical and Reformed Church building, constructed in 1868, a year after the congregation organized on October 28, 1867. In 1916, the current redbrick, Gothic-style church was built at the corner of Sauk Trail and Ash Street; the old church was razed. Charter members of St. Peter's included familiar Frankfort founding fathers like John Bobzin, Benedict Baumgartner, and Fred Leppla.

This postcard of the Frankfort Methodist Church, located at 144 Hickory Street, actually shows the second building owned by the congregation. The original church organized and erected a building in 1856. However, in 1908 the floor gave way during a special service, requiring a complete reconstruction. After 100 years of worshipping in the same location, the Methodists sold to Good Shepherd Lutheran Church and built a new church at the corner of Sauk Trail and Linden Drive.

This postcard of Dr. Walter Hedges' home was taken in the 1920s. Dating back to 1870, the home at 34 West Nebraska Street had some unusual features, according to son Roger, like the stone passageways that ran underground, connecting the house and office. The good doctor dispensed medicine from his own pharmacy at the back of the house. The house and office (later used as a restaurant) burned down in 1987.

This home on the northeast corner of Oak and Oregon Streets was built by merchant Frank Kohlhagen. An interesting combination of Queen Anne and Prairie-style architectures, the home featured decorative wood trim, along with the wide, rectangular front porch supported by Prairie-style columns. In the 1950s, the house was remodeled and the main entrance moved to Oregon Street.

After the 1910 fire, when their livery burned to the ground, the Folkers family rebuilt in brick and installed a motorized elevator in order to make use of the upstairs storage space for the hearse and other vehicles. However, as the need for livery services declined, the automotive business rose. Frankfort residents Adam Heusner and Ben Mager brought their well-established car dealership to the livery building, selling Willys-Overland vehicles, as this 1925 postcard shows.

The Bertha Nieland family home is an expansive American Farmhouse–style dwelling featuring two wings with two entrances and a sturdy quarry stone foundation. While the home has never been moved from its corner spot at Ash Street and Sauk Trail, note that the street signs say Ash and LaPorte Streets, indicating that earlier in history, the short block of Sauk Trail between Ash and Center Streets went by a different name.

In 1925, a modern brick school (pictured) was built in Frankfort for $35,000 on the same property as the original wood-frame schoolhouse. The new school featured three large classrooms, two playrooms, and a large auditorium. In 1938, a full-size gym and auditorium were constructed on the southwest side of the building as part of a Works Progress Administration project in President Franklin Roosevelt's New Deal. As enrollment continued to increase, the original auditorium was converted to two more classrooms, a principal's office was added, and the playrooms became three more classrooms, along with a kitchen. Additional District 157-C schools were built at other locations in 1965, 1975, 1982, and 2006. In 1995, the original grade school was sold, renovated, and renamed Frankfort Founders Center, becoming the home base for the Frankfort Park District.

Joe and Ida Priami ran Frankfort Restaurant—or Joe's, as it was known locally—from the 1920s to the 1940s. Their daughter Kay noted that their meat was always fresh and bought at Folkers Meat Market, two doors down. Joe also made his own chocolate syrup to go with the Meadow Gold ice cream he served, and he made his own "paddle pop," which was a scoop of vanilla ice dream dipped in a maple-flavored coating. After Joe's death, Ida continued the business as Ida's Confectionery (malt shop) until her death in 1961. Ida is pictured here with a customer in the 1930s. (Courtesy of Kay Fredin.)

Frankfort started life as a farm town, so it was not unusual to see livestock in and around the downtown area, even in the 1900s. Here, a herd of pigs makes its way across Kansas Street on the way to the railroad depot and eventually to market. Lifelong resident Happy Bettenhausen recalled seeing cows in their pasture as he walked (or roller-skated) to school down White Street in the 1930s.

This Standard Oil station featured a lunchroom, as well as gas services. It sat at the southeast corner of Route 45 and Route 30 and was owned by the Heusner family. Route 30, also known as Lincoln Highway, was the main thoroughfare between Chicago Heights and Joliet during the first half of the 20th century. Accordingly, the intersection of Routes 45 and 30 in Frankfort offered travelers a variety of food and fuel options over the years.

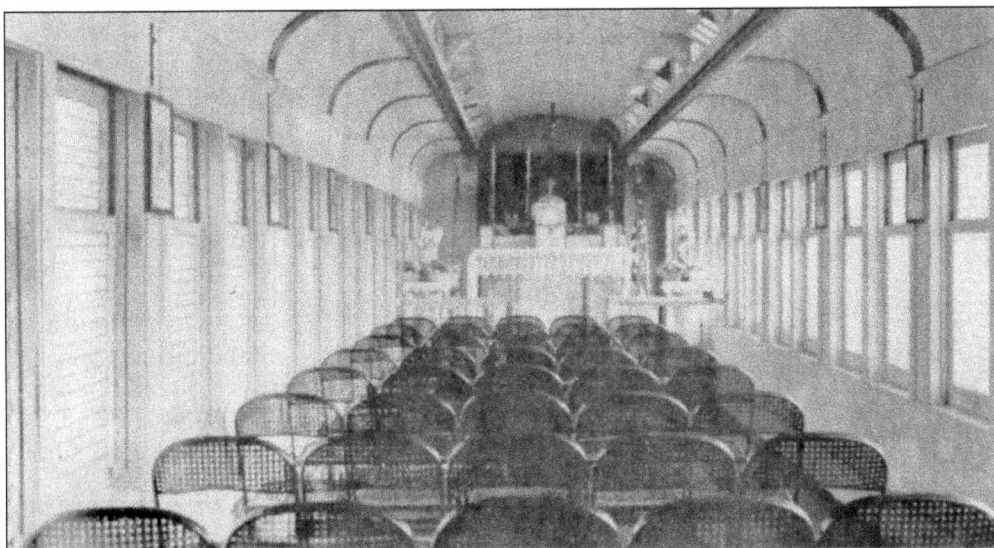
SAINT WILFRID'S CHAPEL--LINCOLN ESTATES, ILL.

Is this a train car or a church? It was both, actually, as residents of the Lincoln Estates neighborhood northeast of Frankfort first met in homes as part of a mission parish. However, in 1936, the Rock Island Railroad donated a retired train car to the congregation. After relocating it from New Mexico and remodeling the interior, the congregation began worshipping at St. Wilfrid's Chapel, called to services by an old brass train bell, a gift from the Elgin, Joliet & Eastern Railway.

The original village hall sat in the shadow of the first wooden water tower, constructed behind it in 1894. The new village hall was built in 1940 just to the east of the original building at Hickory and Kansas Streets; it was home to police and fire stations, pictured here. Although the structure has been extensively renovated and is now home to the Frankfort Chamber of Commerce, the original jail remains tucked away in the back hallway.

Eleven years after St. Wilfrid's bell called its worshippers to service in the train car, St. Anthony Catholic Church celebrated its first mass on September 5, 1948. The new church, located nearby, replaced the old railroad version, purchased for use by a medical center. The old brass train bell, however, became the new bell, which reportedly pealed so loudly during mass that it had to be fully encased in the tower.

Located on the northeast corner of Route 45 and Route 30, the Bobzin and Bennett Gas Station saw its share of travelers through this main crossroads. In this 1947 photograph, a tractor sits behind the building, while Lynn and Nellie Kohlhagen's coupe is parked to the left of the station. The south side of the O'Aces Drive-In is visible on the far left of the scene. An unidentified man works the pump.

The Hedges Clinic was built in 1950 around the existing office of Doctor Hedges. The Hedges home can be seen behind the clinic in this 1955 photograph. The clinic was the result of a revolutionary idea of a small-town doctor who served not just Frankfort, but area residents in a 25-mile radius. Multiple doctors, two dentists, five nurses, and two technicians for the X-ray and laboratory, along with a pharmacist, staffed the new facility. The clinic later moved to its present location at 222 Colorado Avenue, and the original building burned in a 1987 fire. (Courtesy of the Robert Porter Collection.)

Owned by Wayne DePorto, the Frankfort A&W sold root beer for 5¢ in 1950. It could also be purchased in quarts, half gallons, or gallons from this roadside stand located just north of the intersection of Routes 30 and 45. Later remodeled to have the franchise's quirky hat-like brown roof, the A&W was razed to make way for the Frankfort Village Restaurant in the 1970s. (Courtesy of the Robert Porter Collection.)

This 1950s photograph shows the beautiful Gothic-style architecture of St. Peter's Evangelical and Reformed Church, now St. Peter's United Church of Christ. The congregation continues to be part of Frankfort's firm foundation, involved in the community, as well as in wider missions. In the 1950s, St. Peter's had 335 member families, an active men's fellowship, a women's guild, two youth groups, and two choirs. This line drawing was used as an attendance postcard for the St. Peter's Christian Education program to encourage children who had been absent to return to class.

St. Peter's Evangelical and Reformed Church
Frankfort, Illinois

In 1955, Frankfort said good-bye to the Art Bauch Ford and Allis Chalmers dealership (which sold tractors and other vehicles) and hello to Cooper Show Ford. The new Ford dealership was run by well-known Frankfort businessman Ralph Show and was located in the former Joliet and Southern Traction Company building, or trolley barn, at the intersection of Kansas and White Streets. (Courtesy of the Robert Porter Collection.)

This building at 119 Kansas Street has served many purposes over the years, including a general store and post office owned by the Claus Brothers in the 1870s and Robert Stephen from 1914 to 1934. It again served as the post office from 1953 to 1962 until a new mail facility was built at 106 Nebraska Street. Today, it continues as a general store, having experienced a rebirth under owners Jack and Carole Wilger of Frankfort.

The Arch Inn Restaurant, owned by Tony and Jeanette Baker, sat at the corner of Route 30 and Harlem Avenue. Taking advantage of the regular traffic between Joliet and Chicago Heights, the Arch Inn served a specialty called "pheasant chicken," along with steak, shrimp, lobster tail, and Italian spaghetti. The restaurant was in operation from the 1940s to the 1960s.

Originally owned by the Heusner family, the Pilgrim's Rest Motel sat behind the Standard Oil station at the corner of Routes 30 and 45. Ted Massey, a former Standard Oil truck driver took over the property for several years in the 1950s. Massey's service station offered gasoline, diesel fuels, truck tire repair, and "lots of parking space." The motel featured 19 rooms at "commercial" rates and boasted "good restaurants close by."

The Franciscan Sisters of the Sacred Heart live on a beautiful wooded campus along the north edge of Hickory Creek in Frankfort. In 1953, Sacred Heart High School, a residential, all-girls high school, was built for girls considering entering the order. Although the school closed in 1971, and the building has since been razed, the campus now boasts a large chapel, residential housing for aged and infirm sisters, the order's motherhouse, and a retreat center.

The Frankfort Public Library got its start in 1961 when a group of mothers from the Frankfort Parent-Teacher Association decided a library was needed to assist with children's research for school assignments. In March 1962, the group rented this building on the corner of Ash and Nebraska Streets (formerly Zechlin's Furniture) and stocked it with donations from individuals and organizations like the Frankfort Women's Club. The library moved into its present building on Pfeiffer Road in 1979. (Courtesy of the Frankfort Public Library District.)

Frankfort residents have a long history of supporting their community, and the town's park district came into being because of such support. Residents first began raising money in the 1950s to purchase land for a community park. Main Park, located at Nebraska and Locust Streets, was the result of their efforts. The 1974 photograph above shows the eastern view from the playground, looking toward Locust Street (park supporter Eris Rudman's house is behind the row of evergreens). In the photograph below, a Frankfort Park District preschool class poses on the red-and-yellow house-climber, just before Main Park's renovation, complete in 2007. The house-climber has been a perennial favorite for park-goers since the park's early days. Main Park now features a modern playground with multiple slides, swings, and climbers, along with sand volleyball courts, picnic and restroom facilities, and a remote-control car track, situated in between multiple ball fields and the youth football stadium. (Both, courtesy of the Frankfort Park District.)

The Grainery is an iconic landmark in Frankfort, having been a fixture in the community, in one form or another, since 1855. Purchased for $105,000 in 1973 from area farmers who were not interested in keeping the financially troubled business alive, the property (above) was repurposed by Marty and Connie Kaffel. The Kaffels captured the 1890s charm of Frankfort with quaint little shops and cafés fronting wooden sidewalks and cobblestone streets—and all indoors (below). Visible for miles, the 132-foot grain elevator, built in 1945, stands immortalized with an uncommonly spelled name (deliberately done during the renovation to help non-farming folks identify with Frankfort's agrarian roots), yet it is a symbol of home for those who live here.

Like its functional predecessors, however, the Grainery was prone to fire. A blaze in 1984 destroyed several stores, with another 20 suffering some sort of smoke or water damage. Repairs were made, but a second fire in April 1985 burned the 50-year-old building to the ground (above). The concrete elevator built in 1947 survived. Recently, the original seal from the Frankfort Grain Company (left) was donated to the Frankfort Area Historical Society by the family of Wilbert Klier. Used to certify receipts, the seal is the only original artifact that remains from this key piece of Frankfort's early farm history.

Serving an unincorporated area within Frankfort Township, the Frankfort Square Park District was voted into being in 1974 by community residents looking for organized recreational opportunities for their children. Initially operating out of a closet in a local school, the park district, under the continuous leadership of executive director Jim Randall, has expanded over the past 38 years to become a highly visible presence in the area, not only in recreation but in ecological stewardship. The park district's first office and program space, pictured above in 1984, is now the concession stand at the main ball field complex. Below, the recent aerial photograph of the district's administration and program building, which overlooks restored prairie and wetlands—just one part of the 700 acres under their care—shows how the national award-winning park district has matured. Its motto of "Frankfort Square—the friendly park district" ensures that providing quality service to its residents remains the number-one goal and the heart of its operation. (Both, courtesy of the Frankfort Square Park District; below, photograph by Audrey Marquenski.)

Frankfort residents seem to have had a thing for moving train cars. In 1978, Harry D'Ercole Sr., then owner of Enrico's Italian Dining, showed his creative, entrepreneurial side by relocating a caboose and boxcar to his restaurant property on Route 45, just north of Route 30. D'Ercole remodeled both cars and turned them into unique seating areas for patrons. Here, the train cars are shown moving north up White Street onto Route 45 (above) and as part of the restaurant in the 1980s (below). Sadly, construction and reconfiguration of the intersection at Routes 45 and 30 in early 2000 led to the removal of the cars, which now sit on a loyal customer's private property. (Both, courtesy of Harry D'Ercole Jr.)

The 1950s brought the first expansion north and west of the village beyond the downtown area, with the annexation of Lincoln Meadows subdivision. The north unit, named Connecticut Hills, ran along the north side of Route 30 between Elm Street and Cedar Lane. The homeowners had an active neighborhood association, working with the village to improve sewer, water, and road issues in Connecticut Hills, as well as holding "Candidate Nights" and hosting social events. The association was developed in 1965. Connecticut Hills was annexed into the village in 1973.

This 1973 photograph shows Mark's Frankfort Laundry and Ed's Meats & Groceries, both owned by Walter Mark. At the time, the building at Oak and Kansas Streets had been a grocery store for over 100 years, almost without interruption. A few years later, it would become home to Die Bier Stube and Aurelio's Pizza, community favorites until they burned down in 2001. Eventual demolition of the 150-year-old structure at that corner led to the construction of Francesca's Fortunato, an upscale Italian restaurant.

The old Joliet and Southern Traction Company trolley barn served as the location for two automobile dealerships before housing Marquette Auto Parts in the 1970s. In the 1980s, one additional business moved in, a discount office furniture vendor; but by 1996, the building had been vacant for years and had become a home to feral cats. Rescued and renovated by residents Dave and Amy Wilson in 1996, it is again home to local businesses as the two-story Trolley Barn mall.

Built in the late 1970s, Joe and Jeanne Every's ranch home on Larch Road was typical of suburban construction in Frankfort in that era. Modest homes were designed for growing families on spacious quarter-acre lots. The view to the east behind the home shows open farm field, an unusual sight these days except in a few pockets along Frankfort's borders.

Faith Temple, an Assembly of God congregation, got its start in 1979, meeting at Mokena Elementary School for five and a half years, where the founding pastor worked as a custodian until the church was self-supporting and could pay him a salary. The church shown here was built in 1985, and Frankfort residents Art and Jeanette Mark and their daughters were charter members. A missions-minded church, the congregation has since changed its name to International Community Church but still makes its home on Elsner Road.

Another downtown fire in 1987 took out the Alpine Chalet, located at 34 West Nebraska Street. The restaurant occupied the former Hedges Clinic. According to news reports, 75 firefighters from multiple neighboring departments battled the blaze. Damage was estimated at almost half a million dollars, and the structure had to be razed.

After the Frankfort Area Historical Society formally organized in 1972, it used the corner windows in the police department in the former Folkers Livery for historical displays. As the organization grew, it asked the village for assistance in creating a permanent museum space. The far west end of the livery complex was given to the historical society by the village, and renovations began in the early 1980s. The museum now includes display areas, along with a workroom/office and storage area, and is regularly open four days a week to the public.

Located in the former Sippel ice cream parlor, Antiques Unique, owned by Shirley and Dave Walsh, was a Frankfort favorite for more than two decades. Shirley prized her antique inventory as much as her antique building. Her 1979 ad in the *Frankfort Centennial* publication reads: "We guard the past to protect the heritage of our ancestors. Frankfort's well being is in our hands. May we all work to protect Frankfort and its heritage."

This 1986 photograph shows horses tied up outside Kidi's Station, which was one of the many restaurants to occupy the Baumann Tavern after it changed ownership in 1957. Even though she moved to the village in the early 1980s, resident Pamela Biesen remembers the country feel Frankfort had, evidenced by people still riding their horses into town like it was 1880. (Photograph by Pamela Biesen.)

The Grainery fire in 1985 leveled the 1890s-style shopping venue but did not stop the village from repurposing that space with a new retail plaza, anchored by the Always Open convenience store at the east end in the foreground. Notice the path running along the side of the new building. This was the former site of the Michigan Central Railroad tracks and would ultimately become the Old Plank Road Trail bicycle and walking path in the 1990s. Breidert Green is to the left. (Photograph by Pamela Biesen.)

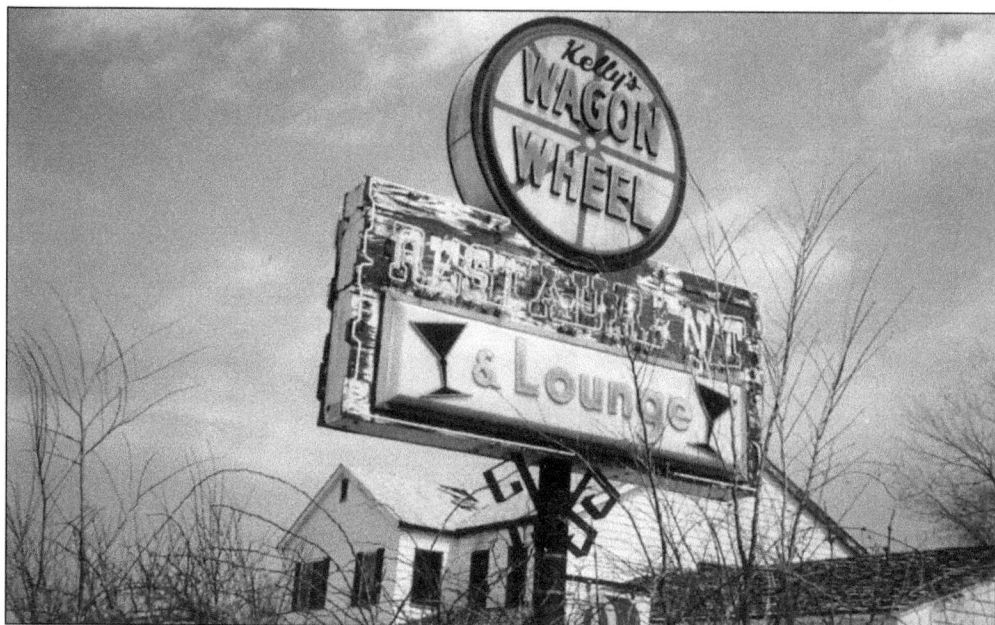

The Wagon Wheel Restaurant and Lounge sat at the corner of Route 45 and Nebraska Street, just west of the current village hall. It was a Frankfort favorite for years, and a 1978 advertisement called it "a small place in the country, with the North woods atmosphere." Ice cream drinks were its specialty, and its lounge provided live entertainment. The restaurant was razed in the 1990s. (Photograph by Pamela Biesen.)

While the Elsner farm endured for 120 years, it, too, disappeared from the Frankfort landscape, and not without a true sense of loss. Anne Helms, curator of the Frankfort Area Historical Society in the 1990s, was quoted as saying, "It's just another thing gone in the name of progress, as they call it." New homes, along with Grand Prairie Elementary School, were built on the site of the former farm.

Three

ALL IN A DAY'S WORK

Good old-fashioned rugged individualism and pioneer spirit led to the creation of many independent businesses in Frankfort's early years. While farmers settled into the fertile lands surrounding town, eager young men invested themselves in providing the goods and services needed for the little village on the prairie. And as times changed, Frankfort residents tried to go with the flow to meet the demands of the people. As in other American communities, however, the Depression took its toll on Frankfort, as did the development of modern shopping malls, which sucked business away from the center of town. But Frankfort never gave up. Its continued efforts to revitalize the historic downtown shopping district, as well as to build up the light industry along the rail lines south of town, have encouraged entrepreneurial thinking and neighbor networking not much different than what the founding fathers were doing 150 years ago. Perhaps the main difference is that the majority of the downtown historic district shops are now run by women, which certainly was not the case in the merchant community of yesteryear but may be creating a new generation of family-run businesses in Frankfort, joining the ranks of Warning Charter Service, Enrico's Italian Dining, Phillips Chevrolet, and others that have survived.

Frankfort started life as a farming community, with county assessor records listing the biggest crops in 1877 as corn, 5,271 acres; oats, 4,822 acres; and timothy meadow (hay), 2,395 acres. In addition, there were over 800 cows kept in Frankfort, which produced 185,150 gallons of milk for sale that year. The Werner family farm implement business, located at 122 Ash Street, provided

much-needed goods and services to these area farmers from 1873 to 1928. Pictured here in 1890 in front of the store, from left to right, are Fred Werner, Freida (Ricka) Werner, unidentified, daughter Ida Werner, and Freida's husband, August Werner. The Werner home stands just to the left of the shop. The warehouse can be seen on the other side of the home.

Johnson Folkers, a Civil War veteran, came to Frankfort in 1863. While he first opened a meat market in town, he later bought out the livery and then the hotel across the street. The livery provided all manner of services, from transportation for visiting musicians needing to get to Warning's Grove to driving the funeral hearse to the area cemeteries. The old wooden livery, pictured here, burned in 1910, destroying almost two dozen horses (including the Folkers children's prize ponies) and devastating the community.

Four blacksmith shops kept Frankfort's horses and farm equipment fully shoed and functional in its early years. Here, unidentified workers pose with their tools outside the shop located at the corner of Oak and Elwood Streets (now Fra-Milco Cabinet Company). This was Henry Eisenbrandt's shop, which he opened after completing an apprenticeship with a C. Eichenberg, according to a family history.

For almost 20 years, the Hickory Creek Creamery Company was a vital part of Will County's thriving dairy industry in the late 1800s. According to county records, the business brought in $10,000 in 1878. In the 1880s, however, the market changed, and it became more profitable to ship milk to the city for processing than to manufacture dairy products on-site. In this photograph, two men, perhaps the Baumgartner brothers, who co-owned the dairy, stand amidst the processing equipment before the creamery closed in 1895.

John Bruggeman owned and operated Bruggeman's Buffet on Kansas Street around the turn of the century. He is pictured here with his trademark handlebar mustache. Notice the ornate woodwork of the bar and the wide assortment of liquor bottles behind it. Baumann's Tavern two doors down only sold beer, whiskey, and highballs—no wine or mixed drinks. Also notice his sign to the right above his head: "If you can't pay, don't play."

Run by Philip Klepper and his son Fred, the Klepper wagon shop was located at 133 Ash Street across from Werner's farm implement business. The pair was said to have been responsible for producing many of the carriages in Frankfort. In 1904, Fred Klepper built a Craftsman home at 133 Walnut Street, where he lived until his death in 1953. The home still features many examples of his excellent woodworking skills.

The Bettenhausen & Knater Harness Shop was located on Ash Street south of Nebraska Street. Here, two unidentified workers pose in their long aprons, dirtied from working with hides to create the leather harnesses. The shop also carried blankets and fly nets: a one-stop shop for horse tack in the 1890s.

Frankfort mailman Henry Fink is pictured here with his daughter Lillie and his wagon horse, Lydia, in the early 1900s. Rural letter carriers served as post offices on wheels, selling stamps and money orders, along with providing other postal services. Rural free delivery (RFD) carriers brought mail to those outside of town, as opposed to in-town residents who picked up their mail wherever the current postmaster (or mistress) was doing business.

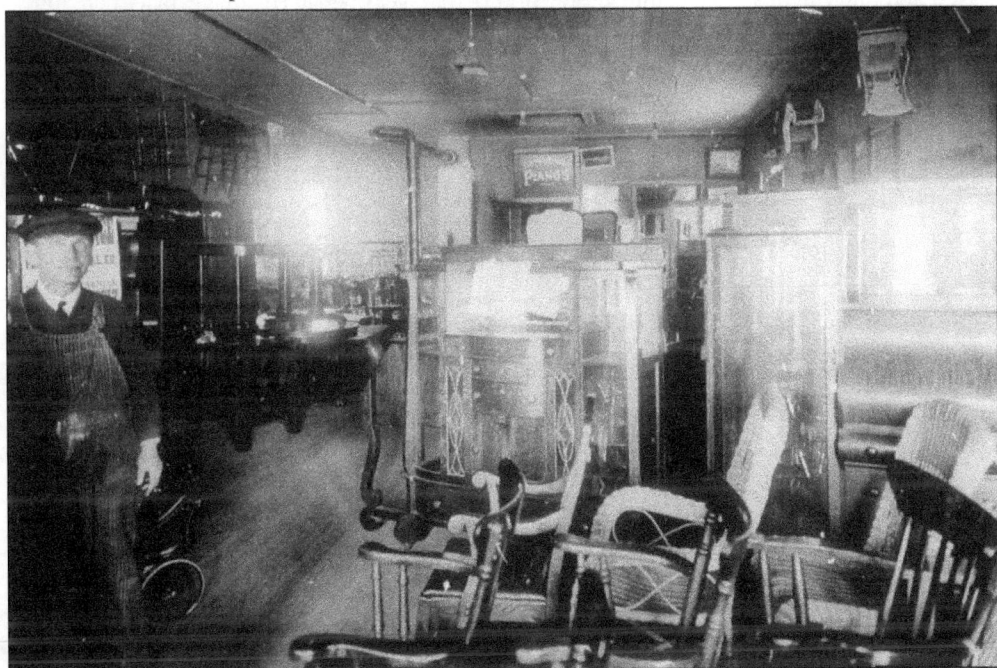

In 1907, Barney Zechlin bought Frankfort's furniture and undertaking business from Ed Hellerman. Reported to be a skilled woodworker and upholsterer, Barney put those gifts to use making lined caskets. A man of many talents, he was also a licensed embalmer, conducting a dozen or so funerals a year. In addition, he kept a bridal registry of sorts, tracking all wedding gifts purchased through him so that no bride received a duplicate gift on his watch. The Zechlin furniture store and casket company was located on the northeast corner of Ash and Nebraska Streets.

The first automobile dealership and garage was located at the corner of Smith and Elwood Streets, which has been known for years as the Blacksmith Shops and was originally the Stephen Brothers wagon and implement shop. Adam Heusner and Ben Mager opened the first garage there in the early 1900s. Pictured here, from left to right, are Henry Heusner, Fred Heusner, Henry Mark, Ben Mager, Adam Heusner, and Charles Peters.

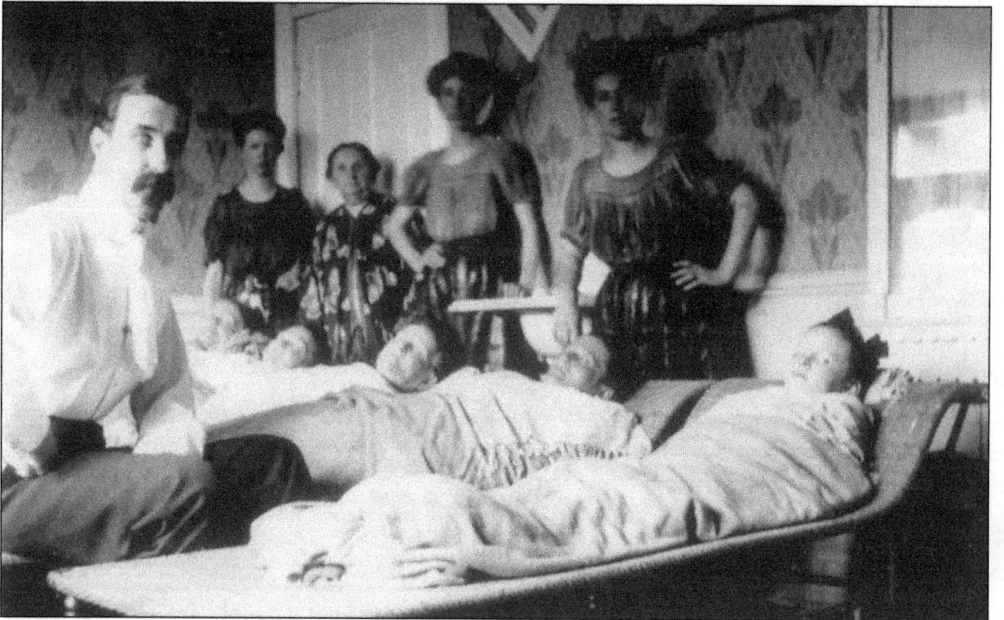

Before the invention and widespread use of antibiotics in the 1940s, illnesses like scarlet fever (basically strep throat and a rash) could be deadly. Here, Doctor Hamlin (seated) treats a room full of patients in a makeshift isolation ward in Art Lambrecht's home, probably around 1912. The only other person identified is Sylvia Pfaff, who would have been a teenager at the time. She is lying on the second cot from the right.

In 1908, the trolley came to town, right down Kansas Street, reaching Chicago Heights by May 1909. Running an east-west route between Aurora and Chicago Heights, the Joliet & Southern Traction Company operated this interurban line for 14 years before the automobile began to replace public transportation. Originally, the company planned a network of interurban lines that would connect Chicago to St. Louis with stops in Bloomington and Pontiac, as well. At its peak, the trolley ran nine round-trips a day between the two end points, which took 3.5 hours to complete. These two pictures were taken on Kansas Street looking west during track construction. Today, the trolley tracks lie buried beneath the asphalt on Kansas Street.

Frankfort Grade School children pose in front of the trolley on Kansas Street, pictured above in 1910. While families might take the interurban to neighboring New Lenox or out to Plainfield to the Electric Park (an amusement park–type venue), the trolley also provided transportation for workers, as well as high school students. The photograph at left shows a 44-ride school ticket for Frankfort resident Vera Staff. Without a high school in town, students wanting to continue their education had to supply their own transportation to Bloom (in Chicago Heights) or Joliet Township High School. Vera attended Bloom and rode the trolley each day to school.

While no further details are given, this group of residents, including Constable William Knippel (second from left in the hat), is conducting a mock trial in the old village hall, prior to 1918. Also pictured, from left to right, are Henry Knippel (the man on trial), Conrad Sippel (a village trustee) and Henry Harnack. Note the potbelly stove to the left and the big wooden door that could close off the jail cells (behind the men).

Margaret Sippel, wife of Conrad, stands behind the marble-topped counter in the family's ice cream parlor in a May 1929 photograph. Note the electric malt mixer next to her and the sundae glasses lined up behind her. The store also sold cigars, as seen in the display case to the right, along with the *Chicago Tribune*. When daughter Katie served as postmistress here from 1934 to 1953, it was rumored that she knew everyone's business because she read everyone's mail.

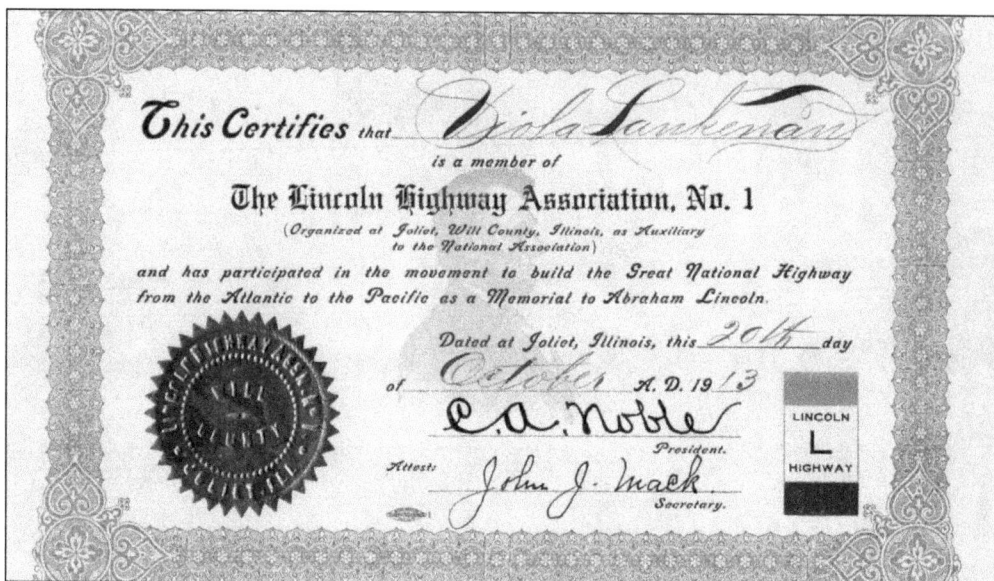

This Certifies that *Viola Lankenau* is a member of

The Lincoln Highway Association, No. 1

(Organized at Joliet, Will County, Illinois, as Auxiliary to the National Association)

and has participated in the movement to build the Great National Highway from the Atlantic to the Pacific as a Memorial to Abraham Lincoln.

Dated at Joliet, Illinois, this *20th* day of *October* A. D. 19*13*

E. A. Noble
President.

Attests: *John J. Mack*
Secretary.

In 1912, Carl Fisher, who built the Indianapolis 500 Speedway, saw the need for a cross-country highway and began lobbying private businesses and individuals to help finance the project. The photograph above shows Frankfort resident Viola Lankenau's certificate, recognizing her membership in the Lincoln Highway Association. While the association never quite realized Fisher's grand goal, it did raise awareness of the need for higher quality roads. Interestingly for Frankfort, though, the highway was originally planned to pass through the heart of the village on the old Sauk Trail; work began on this route in 1914, carried out by an honor camp of inmates from Joliet Prison. The convicts lived in a tent compound one mile east of town on Sauk Trail (below). This free labor force was available thanks to resident Frank G. Folkers's direction of a prisoner rehabilitation program. However, by 1920, when Lincoln Highway was ready to be paved through Frankfort, the route was moved to its current location north of town.

The Thompson farm ran along Route 30 from Locust Street to Elsner Road and north to Colorado Avenue. The majority of the property later became the neighborhood of Connecticut Hills. In this photograph, Konrad Bormet, who worked the farm for the Thompsons, feeds the pigs in the late 1920s. Previously owned by the Sanger family, the farm served as the retirement home and burial place for General Sherman's horse, Sam, after the Civil War.

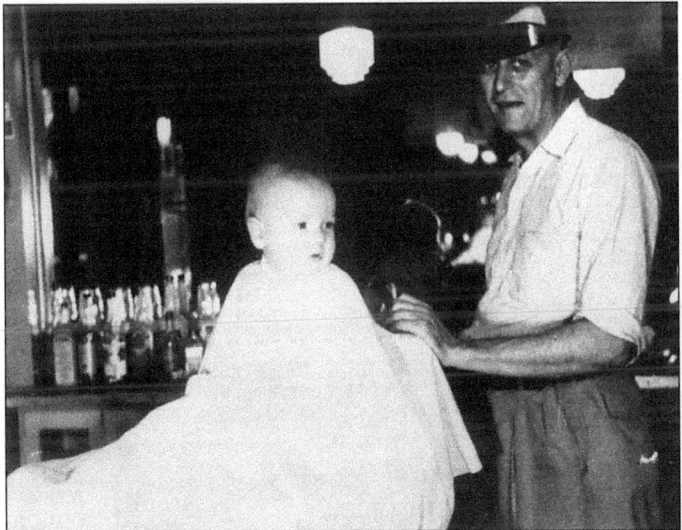

Walter Pfaff is pictured in the shop his father bought upon arriving in town in 1906. A street and a fire station building are named after him for good reason. This virtually lifelong resident served as a barber for 50 years, the village clerk for 50 years, a fireman for 50 years (including chief), a part-time police officer, a water-meter reader, and a village lamplighter (before electricity came to the village in 1913).

Back in 1955, Clarence Waldvogel drove a truck for Capitol Milk. Interestingly, his main competition was brother George, who also drove for Capitol Milk. Here, Clarence is pictured on Hickory Street on the west side of Frankfort Grade School, perhaps getting ready to perform a routine stick test on his load to make sure the separator was working. "Capitol-ize on Health: Drink Capitol Milk" was the company's slogan. (Courtesy of the Robert Porter Collection.)

Charles Baumann was reported to be Frankfort's oldest businessman when he retired at age 91 in 1957. At that time, he said that he had grown tired of the more complicated, modern bookkeeping related to the business. Although Baumann Tavern had been in his family since his grandfather Frederick opened it in 1868, Charles sold to three Frankfort residents—Charles McManimen, Orin Link, and Clarence Heisner.

This 1958 photograph shows Frankfort firefighters promoting a fish fry fundraiser outside the station house located at 123 Kansas. From left to right are Herb Lambrecht, Wendel Morrison, Bob Trump, and Walter Harnack. Frankfort was a volunteer fire department at that time, with approximately 40 members. (Courtesy of the Frankfort Fire Protection District.)

Thanks to the initiative of Frankfort businessman Art Bauch, the Superior Match company—started in Chicago in 1937 by Harold Meitus and his brother Paul—opened a Frankfort production location along the Elgin, Joliet & Eastern Railway in the 1940s. The company focused on selling small orders of one or two cases of matchbooks to rural businesses. Here, unidentified workers pose on the production floor of the factory. (Courtesy of the Robert Porter Collection.)

Camp Manitoqua has been changing lives for over 50 years through its camping and retreat ministry. The Reformed Church Laymen's League purchased 312 acres along Sauk Trail in 1955, and the first summer camp season took place in 1957. This 1968 photograph shows an unidentified camper and counselor, with the swimming pool and dining hall visible behind them. (Courtesy of Camp Manitoqua and Douglas Lee.)

Ed Warning poses here in a 1960s photograph with his original rural mail wagon. Warning served the postal service for 46 years. According to a 1961 *Rockford Register* news article, Warning's route covered 30 miles when he started in 1916. By the time he retired in 1962, his territory had expanded to 69 miles, and he estimated he had delivered more than 500,000 pieces of mail.

This 1970s photograph shows the Frankfort Fire Protection District, which formally organized in 1962, at their station house located where Herschbach Hardware used to be on Kansas Street. At that time, the district covered a 42-square-mile area and had eight pieces of equipment and 50 volunteer firefighters. Today, the district provides services to over 50,000 people in a 50-square-mile area using a full-time career department staffing five stations. (Courtesy of the Frankfort Fire Protection District.)

The Abe Lincoln Motel was built in 1958 by Joe and Judy Kordik, along with Joe's brother Bill and their parents, Rose and Joe Kordik. The Abe Lincoln featured 12 air-conditioned units, wall-to-wall carpeting, and free in-room television. The motel served travelers along busy Lincoln Highway, as well as visitors to Valley View Farms, a tourist destination located just west of the property. After Joe Jr.'s death, Judy ran the motel with her daughters Jodi and Cindy until the sale of the property in 2006. (Courtesy of Jodi Gallagher-Dilling.)

From 1965 to 1974, Ted Massey (front left) served as police chief of a department that was created when the first village constable was hired in 1879. Early responsibilities for the constable included cutting weeds, keeping the fire going in the village hall, and housing tramps overnight in the jail. Almost a century later, Frankfort still did not have a dedicated police station, and officers on night duty answered the police phone in their homes. Chief Massey made organizational changes, hiring enough part-time officers to have police coverage around the clock and arranging for the police department to have an assigned room in the back of the village hall. Under his leadership, additional full-time officers were added. Pictured here, from left to right, are (first row) Chief Amos "Ted" Massey and Walt Johnson; (second row) Robert Porter, Ron Reed, Wayne Mangun, Jim Walker, Virgil Coleman, and Jimmy Warren. (Courtesy of the Frankfort Police Department.)

Four

THE TIES THAT BIND

Over the years, friendships and family ties formed in Frankfort have a way of enduring, no matter where life takes residents or what it brings. From childhood friends who still correspond with each other at the age of 85, to women who can say they are 50-year members of the Frankfort Women's Club, to Frankfort grade school and high school class reunions, to a town that pitches in to run a nationally ranked Labor Day festival each year, there is something about Frankfort that enables people to say about their hometown, "It's the nicest place I know."

Former Frankfort resident Dale Reils affirmed this in a letter written to the Frankfort Area Historical Society in 2008 after the death of his parents, Clyde and Luella Reils, in a tragic natural gas explosion. The letter was published in an FAHS newsletter, and the following excerpt reveals much about Frankfort's character:

> Several months ago, I wrote a letter to the Frankfort Area Historical Society describing what life was like growing up in Frankfort in the 1940s and 1950s. In the letter, I tried to describe all the things that I felt the community and my family contributed to my upbringing. The letter concluded with the question, "Do the village fathers and the residents of Frankfort have the same morals and objectives with our kids today that our parents and leaders had back then?" That question was answered for me on September 6, 2008. At 5:30 in the morning, there was a terrible explosion that took the lives of both my parents . . . We have started the healing process. I doubt we will ever be back to what we consider normal. A big part of our lives is gone. But, thanks to our friends and neighbors and the police and firemen, we still have some special memories to cling to. If there was ever a doubt in my mind about the community of Frankfort and the dedication of its people to each other, I have none now.

Music played an important role in the village, from the creation in 1875 of the Frankfort Germania Saengerbund, a German singing society, to the formation of multiple community bands. Pictured here are the Frankfort Cornet Band (above), which dates back to 1881, and the Frankfort Brass Band (below), which dates back to 1897. Both groups were active in the community and likely performed in Union Hall, a gymnasium used for athletic and performing events at that time. Union Hall was located directly south of the Folkers Livery. Musical groups also used Woodmen Hall on Ash Street for performances around the turn of the century. Thanks to resident Frank Folkers, the Frankfort Area Historical Society Museum now owns one of the original horns from the 1897 Brass Band.

This 1905 flyer (right) lists an Independence concert "arranged and managed" by the Frankfort Brass Band, preceded by a parade led by the band. With a love for music carrying across generations of Frankfort residents, the 1897 Brass Band reorganized in 2004. Under the leadership of John Herder, the band (pictured below on the stage in the old Frankfort Grade School gymnasium) currently plays at many community events, including the Frankfort Preservation Foundation Ice Cream Social and the Frankfort Fall Festival Labor Day parade. It is a community band in the true sense of the word, drawing from all ages and experience levels, all for the love of music and community spirit.

IN DE PEN

d-ence Day Celebration for 1905

AT

FRANKFORT,

arranged and managed by the

Frankfort Brass Band

will be held at

Froehner's Park

PARADE

of the principal streets of the Village by the Band, in the morning.

BAND CONCERT

at the Park after 12:00 noon.

RACES AND CONTESTS

Men's Races		Ladies' Races	
Free-for-all	1.50	Free-for-all Girls	1.00
Fat Man's	2.00	Girls under 12	.50
Boys' Races		" 12 to 18	.75
Free-for-all	1.00	Fat Woman's	2.00
Boys under 12	.50		
" 12 to 15	.75	Boys 15 to 20	.75
Wheel-barrow Race	1.00	Three-legged Race	.75
Bag Race	.75	Pie-eating Contest	1.00
TUG OF WAR, Teams of 6 men			**$5.00**

Base Ball Game postponed

Balchowsky's department store was quite a modern novelty at the time it was built in 1887. Yet, like many modern developments, farmland stood just outside its back door. Here, Caroline Baumann, Arthur Hollstein, and Stella Krusemark play with a heifer in the pasture behind the store at the corner of Ash and Kansas Streets.

Frankfort's small-town values led to long-lasting friendships, especially among those who helped build the town from the ground up. Pictured here, probably in the mid-1880s, are young men from many of the founding families. They are, from left to right, (seated) Peter Folkers, unidentified, and Otto Herschbach; (standing) Henry August "Gus" Baumann, unidentified, George Haass, and two unidentified.

On March 26, 1899, these young men and women made their confirmation at St. Peter's Evangelical and Reformed Church under the guidance of Rev. Gustave Lambrecht. Pictured, from left to right, are (first row) Gustie Maue, Frances Andres, Anna Bauch, Emma Kuhn, and Sadie Damann; (second row) George Elsner, Carrie Hohenstein, Frank Rehberg, George Hellerman, Charles Peters, Ed Stauffenberg, Elizabeth Weitendorf, William Wischover, and Reverend Lambrecht; (third row) Arthur Kohlhagen, Arthur Beckstein, Henry Bruggeman, Arthur Stauffenberg, Henry Haake, and Emil Hinspeter.

Around the turn of the century, the village's Fourth of July parade offered Barney Zechlin the chance to show off his family and his business on a float. Note the beautiful wood rockers and cabinets displayed on the wagon. Barney also sold washing machines and musical instruments, along with handcrafted wood furniture and caskets. Evelyn and Louise Zechlin, Barney's teenage daughters, sit on either side of wagon driver Pete Hansen; the others are unidentified.

In the early 1900s, roads were just beginning to evolve from their rutted dirt existence. Nevertheless, Colonel Lyman and his friend and Frankfort resident Charles Pfaff used to ride their bicycles from Frankfort to Chicago and back. From left to right are an unidentified boy, Walter Pfaff, Sylvia Pfaff (on father's bicycle), Charles Pfaff, Colonel Lyman, and an unidentified girl.

As previously mentioned, music was very much a part of Frankfort residents' lives. More proof of that is seen in this photograph, taken around 1910 on Kansas Street, of Emma Sippel (far right in front of trolley) and her many, many piano students. Note that the third girl in the back row on the left is Viola Lankenau; she went on to become a teacher and administrator for Frankfort Grade School.

The Modern Woodmen of America organized in Frankfort in 1895. A fraternal insurance organization, they paid out death benefits to members' kin, as well as providing a source of community entertainment in their lodge near the corner of Ash and Nebraska Streets. Concerts, dances, social gatherings, and basketball games often took place in Woodmen Hall.

It looks like half the town turned out for Willie Green's birthday party on the lawn of his family home on Nebraska Street. Pictured, from left to right, are (first row) Eloise Kohlhagen, Olive Kohlhagen, Evelyn Pfaff, and baby ? Craig; (second row) Grace Kohlhagen, Dorothy Herschbach, Esther Hall, Eveyln Zechlin, Marcia Craig, Lester Koerner, Virginia Craig, Sarah Balchowsky, Walter Herschbach, and Roy Koerner; (third row) Sylvia Pfaff, Mildred Stephen, Ada Eichmeier, Mildred Walsh, Bernice Zechlin, Gordon Craig, birthday boy Willie Green, Margaret Stephen, and Robert Herschbach; (fourth row) Clarence Folkers.

Frankfort has had the love of the game for over 100 years. Adult baseball teams played competitively against other area towns, with spectators actually betting on the games—sometimes thousands of dollars. Pictured around 1910, from left to right, are residents (first row) Walter Pfaff and Eugene Walsh; (second row) ? Morgan, Henry Breidert, Albert Pfaff, Roy Stevens, and John Fox; (third row) Al Zechlin, Frank Eisenbrandt, Bill Koerner, Fred Krusemark, George Haass, Eddie Topp, and Walden Larsen.

The seventh and eighth grade class of 1915 poses on the porch of classmate Miriam Balchowsky's house. Pictured from left to right are (first row) Adeline Eichmeier and teacher Howard Craig; (second row) Mable Block, Florence Folkers, Mable Eisenbrandt, Bernice Zechlin; (third row) Milton Heisner, Miriam Balchowsky, Grace Kohlhagen, Vera Nieland, Christina Guether, and Ezra Marti.

From generation to generation, Frankfort friendships are the ties that bind. Pictured above, from left to right, are playmates Henry Heusner, Frank Folkers, George Folkers, Richard "Dick" Lambrecht, and George E. Sangmeister in front of the Folkers Livery, perhaps in the midst of a game of cops and robbers in the mid-1930s. About that same time, the friends gathered at Dick Lambrecht's house for his birthday, mugging for the camera while stacked on a ladder. Pictured from bottom to top are Dick Lambrecht, George Folkers, Henry Heusner, Frank Folkers and future Frankfort US congressman George E. Sangmeister. Arthur Lambrecht, Dick's father, stands to the right. Though the miles separated them after they grew up and left Frankfort, they remained fast friends, staying in touch with each other and the Frankfort Area Historical Society over the years.

Born on Valentine's Day, Isabella Gaines, granddaughter of Frankfort businessman August Werner, did not marry until much later in life, around age 50. She did, however, receive a multitude of valentines over the years as a primary teacher for Frankfort Grade School. Her extensive valentine collection was bequeathed to the Frankfort Area Historical Society in her will and is put on display every February. Pictured here is a special teacher valentine given to Isabella by a student in the 1920s.

Before the addition of the gymnasium at Frankfort Grade School in 1938, community-organized teams played basketball games in the old Woodmen lodge, just two blocks from the school. This 1922 team is the first school basketball team and features players, from left to right, (first row) Lawrence Dietrich and Burton Breidert; (second row) coach and principal B.C. Solomon, Edmund Ebert, Floyd Lankenau, and Walter Herschbach; (third row) Lester Koerner, Leroy Mager, Carl Baumann, and Harold Ebert.

From left to right, Richard Lambrecht, George Folkers, Frank Folkers, and Henry Heusner pose with their instruments in their Frankfort Grade School band uniforms around 1940 in front of the Folkers Livery. Frank recalled that he and his brother were given horns to play because piano lessons "didn't work out," as he put it. Likely made before 1900, Frank's original baritone is on display at the Frankfort Area Historical Society Museum.

Basketball was not just for boys. Here, the 1937 Frankfort Grade School girls' team poses for the camera on the outdoor court on school grounds. From left to right are (first row) Jeanette Heusner, Arlene Janssen, and Adeline Janchow; (second row) Virginia Warning, Jeanette Eisenbrandt, Marjorie Bauch, and unidentified.

The first building in the Summit Hill School District 161 was located south of Route 30 on Eightieth Avenue and served the surrounding Frankfort township area. In 1938, Ruth Geuther taught this group of third grade students, pictured from left to right: (first row) Daniel Hecht; (second row) Lloyd Bettenhausen, Wade Krohn, Betty Vernon, Gene Krohn, Dale Krohn, Ruth Bettenhausen, Glen Krohn, Homer Hanrahan, and Lois Bettenhausen; (third row) Dorothy Young, Dorothy Bettenhausen, Chuck Vernon, Bernadine Bolin, Laverne Strassenberg, Naomi Bolin, Lorraine Bettenhausen, and Roy Ebert.

Twins Alan and Roger Hedges grew up in Frankfort as the sons of the town doctor. Pictured here at their birthday party in 1939 are, from left to right, (first row) Henry Heusner, Alan Hedges, and Roger Hedges; (second row) Lynn Kohlhagen, Kathryn Lambrecht, Dick Lambrecht, Janet Folkers, and George Sangmeister Jr. (Courtesy of the Hedges Collection.)

Warning's Grove, along with Geuther's Grove, was a place to go for picnics, dances, baseball games, and other social events. Located along the east side of Route 45, south of Hickory Creek, the grove's remaining woods could no doubt tell some tales. Pictured at a Hobo Party, from left to right, are (first row) Katherine Warning, Della Tinker, Ida Andrew, Minnie Clark, Blanche Mitchell, Lee Breidert, Mary Pfaff, and Irma Hedges; (second row) Emma Scott, Edith Heusner, Alan Hedges, Roger Hedges, and Elsa Warning.

The cast of a Mother Goose production lines up across the stage for its final bow in the Frankfort Grade School gymnasium in 1941. The gymnasium was considered to be one of the finest in the area, with built-in wooden bleachers rising up to the ceiling opposite the stage. All manner of school and community events took place in the gym over the years, including roller-skating. Organized by police officer Virgil Coleman and his wife, Lola, and run by the Frankfort Police Department, this Friday-night, school-year activity was a favorite among Frankfort youth for many years. (Courtesy of the Hedges Collection.)

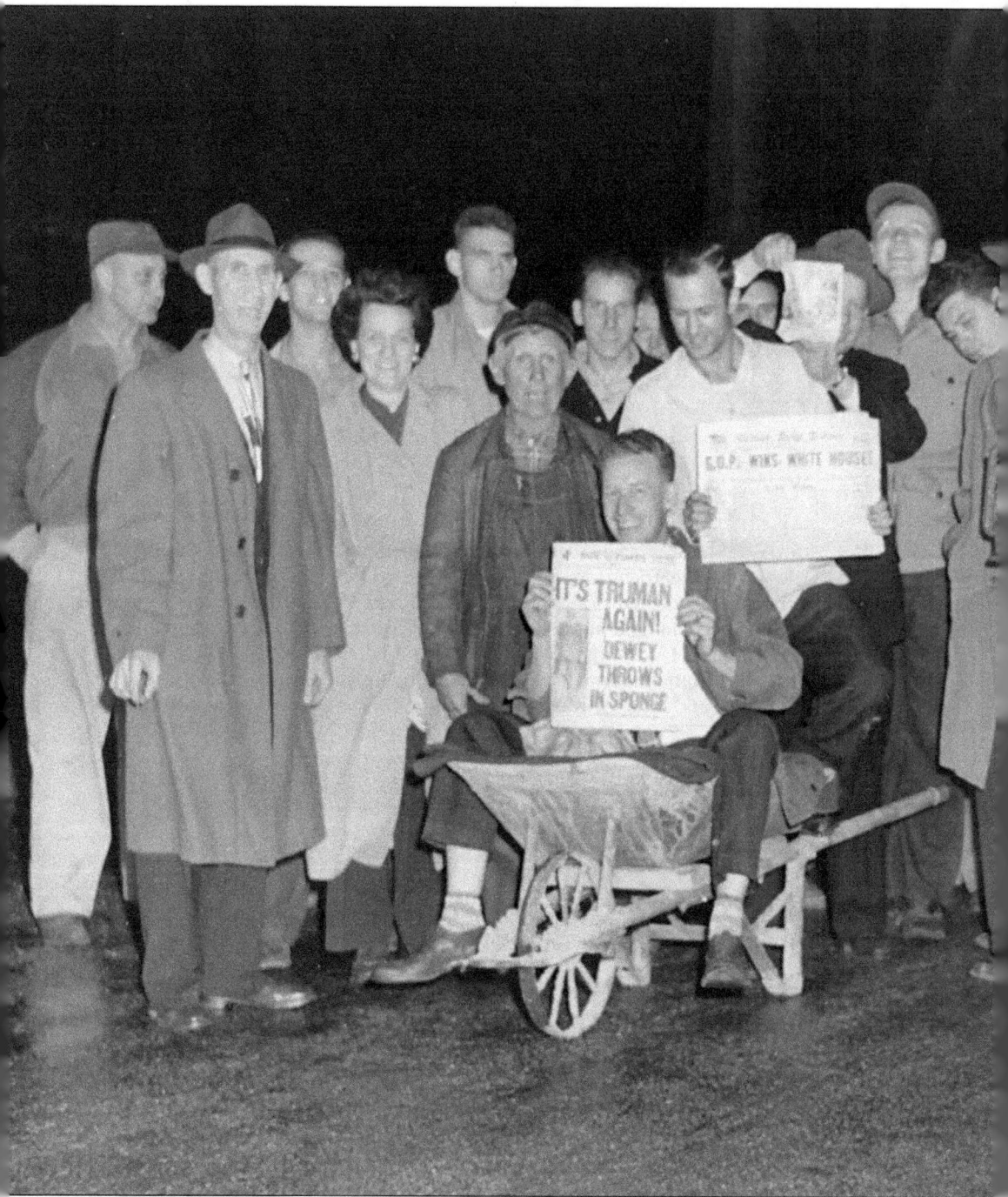

Frankfort has long been a Republican-leaning town. However, one of its two 30-year-term mayors, George C. Sangmeister (front left) was as Democratic as they come. His son, George E., followed in his father's footsteps as three-term a Democratic US congressman. However, this charming community photograph shows residents gathered on the night after the 1948 election and the infamous "Dewey Defeats Truman" headline, smiling for the camera in spite of the news of another four years of a Democrat in the White House. In a 1993 letter written to the Frankfort

Area Historical Society, longtime resident Henry Heusner recalled: "Why, I even had a dog my dad named Dewey. He hated Democrats—my dad, not my dog—but then, the entire town hated Democrats, which brings me to the unexpected phenomena which had Democrat George Sangmeister Sr. reelected as mayor time after time!" Nort Blaylock sits in the wheelbarrow holding up one newspaper with the correct headline, while ? Morgan stands behind holding an incorrect edition. Constable Fred Breymeyer holds the lantern. Other townspeople are unidentified.

This 1940s photograph was taken from the rooftop of Grayce's Frankfort Tavern at 113 Kansas Street. Mayor George Sangmeister leads the parade, followed by the Matteson American Legion Parade Post No. 474. The parade is headed west on Kansas Street, likely to the village hall, where it would stop for a brief ceremony honoring the servicemen and dedicating a service flag.

This photograph depicts one of Frankfort's long-standing community traditions: the annual Memorial Day parade in the downtown area, followed by a ceremony at the village hall, and a trip out to Pleasant Hill Cemetery. The mayor would read the names of the war veterans, and then the schoolchildren would sing "Cover Them with Flowers" and place a bouquet on each grave before heading back to the school grounds for refreshments.

Minnie Elsner formed the Amite Club in 1915 with 12 members. The name was derived from the French word *amitié*, which means "friendship." The women met every two weeks in a member's home, alternating service projects with sewing projects. Pictured here at a 1950s-era Christmas party are, from left to right, (seated) Beulah Kohlhagen, Minnie Elsner, Elsna Warning, Hilda Lambrecht, Viola Lankenau, Clara Pfeiffer, Elenore Weitendorf, and Clara Kohlhagen; (standing) ? Bizer, Lou Breidert, Lizzie Wischover, Betty Heisner, Edith Heusner, and Mary Pfaff. (Courtesy of the Robert Porter Collection.)

In 1953, St. Peter's Evangelical and Reformed Church set a new cornerstone in the addition of the educational annex. The new space included a kitchen, office, lounge, choir room, and 16 classrooms. Pictured here, from left to right, are Ernie Knuteson, Donald Schroeder, Rev. Erich Bizer, and unidentified. (Courtesy of the Robert Porter Collection.)

In 1955, Frankfort celebrated its birth with a huge centennial festival. Spanning five days, the event included the Centennial Queen's Ball, a tea and fashion show, a carnival (above), four performances of a historical pageant entitled *Frankfort Through the Years*, historical window displays, a milking contest, a speech by Sen. Everett Dirksen, two parades, and a Sunday-morning service featuring the Centennial Choir. The Women's Club was also given authority during the festival to fine anyone not in an authentic 1890s costume. The funds raised from this event were put toward the purchase of land for a community park. The members of the Historical Program Committee (below) are hard at work. They are, from left to right, Frances Breidert, Burton Breidert, chairman Ada Lambrecht, and Viola Lankenau.

As a 15-year-old organization with 52 members, the Frankfort Lions Club sponsored a float in the centennial parade. Over the years, the Frankfort Lions involved themselves in community improvement projects like installing gas lines at Frankfort Grade School and moving the playground equipment, paying for street signs in the village, installing lights at the main park, and supporting the Little League teams. Former resident Albert Krusemark I is the last remaining founding Lion. He will be 97 in 2012 and has since retired to Florida.

These members of the Frankfort Women's Club are enjoying themselves at the Centennial Tea and Fashion Show. Pictured, from left to right, are (first row) Irma Hedges, Mary Pfaff, and unidentified; (second row) Marie Peterson, Lois Shoen, unidentified, Emma Scott, and Leila Folkers. The Women's Club was also responsible for making and selling centennial dolls, which generated over $1,800 in profits.

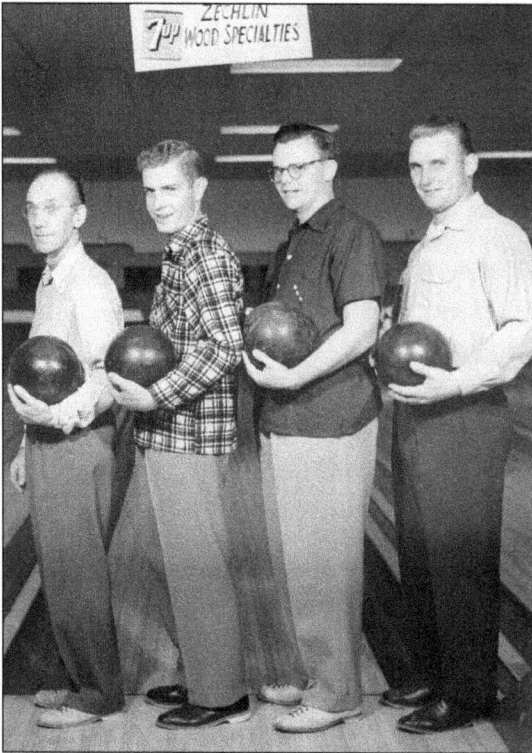

In 1947, a bowling alley opened in what was once the second floor of B. Balchowsky & Sons department store at Ash and Kansas Streets. Some Frankfort residents still remember the hand-set pins of the six-lane alley. Here, members of a Thursday night league team pose for the camera. From left to right are Al Zechlin, John Fedak, Clarke Bennett, and Clarence Harms. As of 2012, the Frankfort Bowl is still operational and a favorite spot for local residents.

Volunteer fireman Walter Pfaff sits at the wheel of the village's first Model T fire truck, which he rescued from the scrap heap by purchasing it from the fire department for $10 in 1955. A charter member of the department when it was formed in 1922, Pfaff originally drove the Model T engine home from Chicago after its purchase for $2,550 in 1923. After buying it for himself, Pfaff replaced hose reels with benches and liked to give Frankfort children an exciting ride down memory lane.

In 1968, Frankfort helped Illinois celebrate its sesquicentennial during the annual fall festival. Here, Frankfort's mayor Glenn Warning presents an official proclamation to Ralph Show, president of the chamber of commerce, which sponsored the celebration. Ralph is behind the wheel of a restored 1931 Model A Ford station wagon owned by Frankfort resident Paul Lambrecht.

Frankfort loves its heritage celebrations, and the birthday of the United States of America was no exception. Here, the Frankfort Area Historical Society's Fall Festival float follows a patriotic theme for the 1976 bicentennial parade. From left to right are Melissa Heyne, Cathy Heyne, Museum curator Anne Helms, and Barbara Stellon. The driver is Matt Mantia.

Before Frankfort Fall Festival, there were Sauerkraut Days, sponsored first by the chamber of commerce in 1961 and then by the Frankfort Lions Club, beginning in 1963. The Lions renamed the festival Sauerkraut and Wiener Day. As the first year's sauerkraut had reportedly been too sour to eat without adding lots of sugar, the Lions went looking for a new and improved recipe. They found it in the files of fellow Lion and restaurateur/chef Tony Baker (right), who owned the Arch Inn at Route 30 and Harlem Avenue in Frankfort. Baker became the event's head chef for the next six years. Also pictured in this publicity shot for the fundraiser are taste-testers Rev. Jim Parker of Frankfort United Methodist Church (left) and local pharmacist Bob Dean. (Courtesy of the Robert Porter Collection.)

While this candid photograph captures an afternoon of lighthearted summer fun among friends in the Krusemark pool, it shows only one side of the members of the Frankfort Women's Club. Formed in 1917 and still in existence in 2012, the club first organized as the Frankfort Home Improvement Club and primarily provided help with the war effort. Despite a few name changes and a six-month hiatus, the Frankfort Women's Club has endured, continuing to live out its mission to "study social science of the home, inspire culture and cordial relations among women, and to contribute to the general welfare of the community." Over the years, the club has provided extensive financial support to the local schools, the Red Cross, the March of Dimes, and other charities and continues to be involved in social, educational, and philanthropic pursuits.

With its German heritage continuously woven throughout the fabric of the village, reestablishing ties with Frankfurt am Main, Germany, seemed only natural. In 1972, Robert Harlan, American consul general to Frankfurt am Main, approached the village about being the American representative in Frankfurt's annual Schlossfest (Castle Festival). Conversations and planning continued for months with Harlan, who was serving as the German festival's president; and in June 1973, a group of Frankfort residents traveled to Germany to participate in this cross-cultural event. At the 1,000-year-old Hoechst Castle, the Frankfort delegation viewed a display of gifts and mementos sent by hometown businesses, organizations, and churches and received an official royal welcome. Pictured discussing the upcoming trip are (seated) chamber of commerce president Herman Fabiani; (middle) project chair Fran Breidert; (back, from left to right) Mayor Glenn Warning, Consul General Robert Harlan, and FAHS acting president Don Witt.

Happy Bettenhausen developed a love for the accordion from his Aunt Alma, who passed along a Hohner two-row, button box accordion to her eight-year-old nephew. Happy learned to play by ear and used to play special events and parades. Later, in the 1970s, he became a regular entertainer on Sunday afternoons at Chef Klaus's restaurant. From left to right are Helmut Krohn on drums, Happy's son Leroy Bettenhausen on banjo, and Happy Bettenhausen with the accordion.

With the library in tight rental quarters on the corner of Ash and Nebraska Streets, staff made the most of the vacant lot on Ash Street, bringing children outside for summer story-time sessions. The note on this photograph says that the boys did not want to participate in the game. The view looking east shows White Street from the grassy area just north of the Ash Street building.

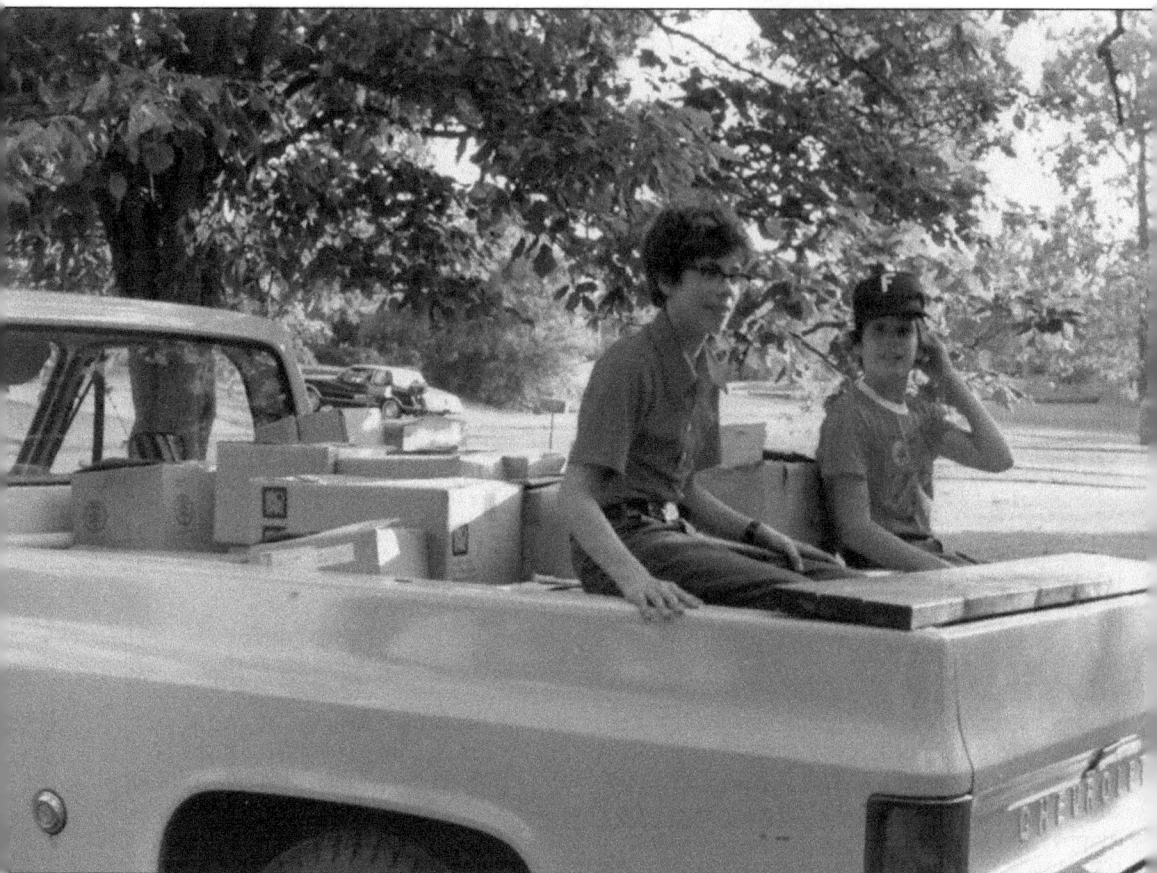

Moving day for the library came in 1979. A community effort, trucks were borrowed from individuals and organizations like the Frankfort Square Park District. Books were boxed and loaded into the backs of pickups, along with the helpers, who kept an eye on things for the two-mile jaunt to the new location on Pfeiffer Road. Over the years, the library has expanded its floor space and added an outdoor sculpture garden and terrace. The Friends of the Library continue to support the library's growth, much like the original volunteers. Pictured on the truck are Warren Weiss (left) and Mike Phillips.

Frankfort News, started by resident Eris Rudman, was a 23-year tradition in Frankfort, delivered to each village resident free of charge. It contained monthly news and notes from the village and local organizations, as well as other interesting tidbits. Eris's crew of volunteers worked to format, print, fold, stuff, and mail the newsletter. Production stopped in 1996 with Eris's death. Volunteers are, from left to right around the table, Betty Holman, Dorothy Porter, Marilyn McManimen, Freida Schultz, and Irene Scheer.

Driving south on Route 45 past Nebraska Street, the Gas City cow stood watch over town for over 35 years. The giant black-and-white bovine came to live in Frankfort in 1976. Originally, Gas City owner Bill McEnery had placed the cow on the roof of his first gas station at Fifty-fifth and Pulaski Streets in Chicago, to advertise that he sold milk (unusual for a gas station in the 1970s). However, the roof gave way, and the cow was relocated to a home in the Frankfort countryside. Business developments in 2012 forced a second move for the cow, now at home at an ice cream shop in neighboring Mokena.

As with many historical structures, people do not often realize their significance until they are gone, which is what happened with Frankfort's Michigan Central Railroad depot, torn down in 1961. Over the next two decades, however, residents realized the importance of the railroad to Frankfort's early development and identity and erected a new depot as the focus of a downtown park named Burton Breidert Village Green, or Breidert Green to locals. Pictured here at the dedication of the village green are former police chief Ted Massey and Joyce Petnuch, flanked by two unidentified young girls in German costumes.

As further proof of Frankfort's commitment to historical preservation, the Frankfort Area Historical Society Time Machine program brought living history demonstrations into Frankfort classrooms from 1986 to 1992. The society won an award from the Congress of Illinois Historical Societies and Museums for its educational efforts in 1987. Pictured here is volunteer Maridell Condon working with a kindergarten class at Chelsea School.

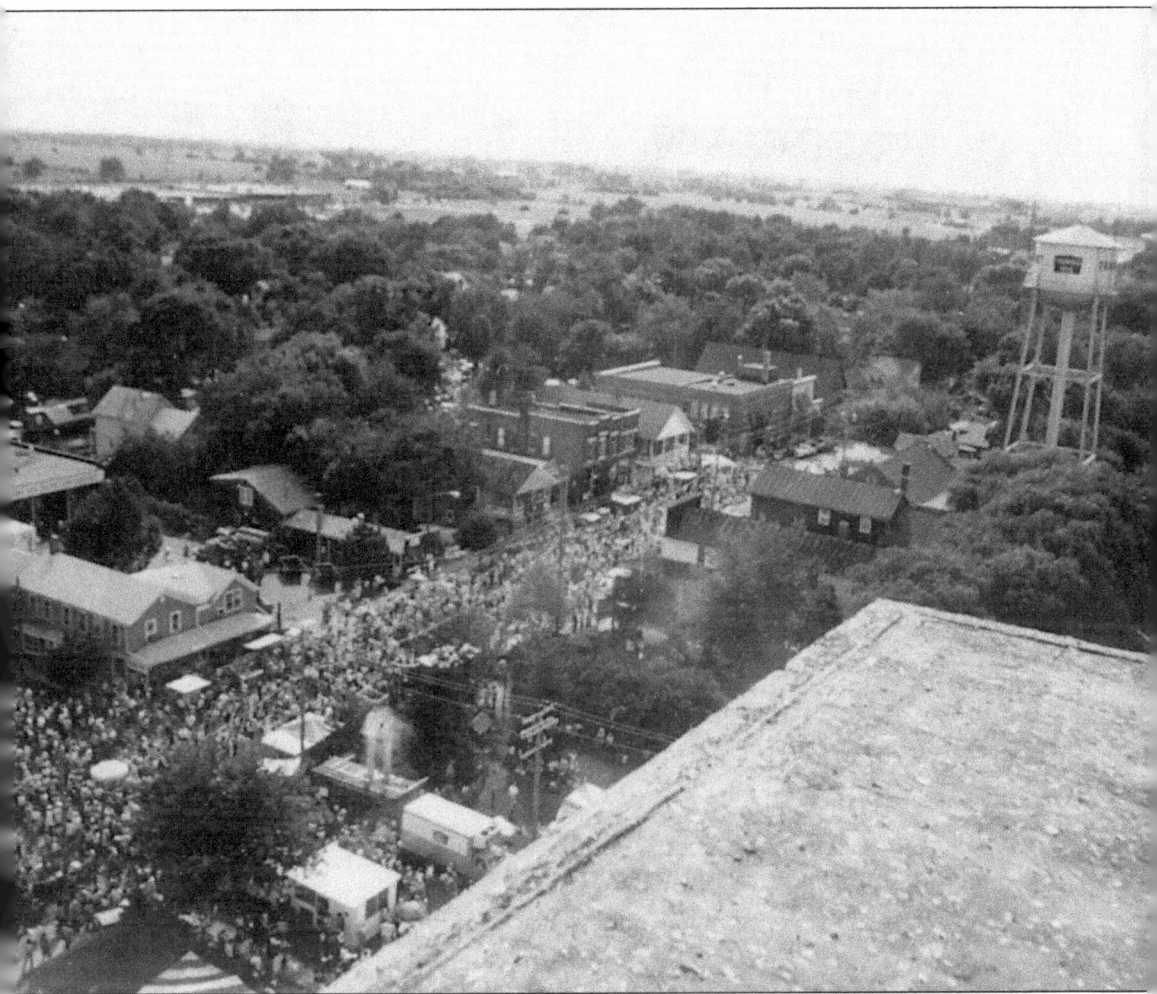

This aerial photograph of Frankfort Fall Festival was taken by police officers from the top of the Grainery tower, probably in the 1980s. The heavily wooded area behind the buildings is the downtown residential district south and west of Kansas Street, which is visible in the foreground and filled with fest-goers. Folkers Hotel and the old Folkers Livery can be seen at the end of Kansas Street to the far right. (Courtesy of the Frankfort Police Department.)

Frankfort Fall Festival continues to draw 200,000–300,000 people each Labor Day weekend. Artisan craft booths line the streets for shoppers. A carnival entertains the children, while live music entertains the adults from noon to midnight. Another highlight of the weekend is the parade on Sunday afternoon. In this photograph, the Frankfort Grade School Tiger Band (now known simply as Frankfort Tiger Band) marches in the parade down Ash Street. This is a pre-1985 photograph because the Grainery shops are still visible in the background.

In this 1987 photograph, a group of Frankfort Fall Festival volunteers, along with fire department staffer Ralph Eisenbrandt (left center), chats as the festival breakdown takes place around them at the end of the weekend. From left to right are (front) an unidentified boy, Bob Murphy, and Cheryl Howard (back to the camera); (back) Ralph Eisenbrandt, an unidentified man, and Ann Karyn Eisenbrandt. (Photograph by Pamela Biesen.)

The Frankfort Lions Club raised funds for its service projects in many different ways over the years. From turtle races to selling cookware to Lions candy days, the club worked hard to earn money to give back to those in need. In 1982, the Frankfort Lions took a new approach, raffling off a new car at their annual dance held the night before Frankfort Fall Festival opened. The first year they gave away a Chevrolet Chevette. Soon after, they began raffling off Cadillacs and eventually moved to a split-the-pot cash prize. Pictured here in front of the old O'Aces Drive-In (seen in the cover photograph) in 1985 are, from left to right, Lions Mike Rafacz, Sam Giordano, Les Egbert, Gus Anagnos, and Dutch Deckleman. (Courtesy of Les Egbert.)

Peace Community Church has strong roots in the Frankfort community, organizing as a church plant in the former Heritage Hall (now LaSalle Street Securities) in 1977. The congregation began worshipping at Camp Manitoqua in 1978. This photograph shows Peace Community Church in 1999, just 12 years after the congregation broke ground for their own building in 1987. The church continues to be a vital force in Frankfort, offering a large sanctuary, a gym, an educational wing, a library, and a preschool. (Photograph courtesy of Peace Community Church.)

Carl Lindee (pictured below riding east on Kansas Street on his antique bike) and his wife, Maggi, loved Frankfort and its sense of history. While they both got involved with the Frankfort Area Historical Society, Carl also formed the Frankfort Car Club in 1976, where the focus was antique cars. The first major event the club hosted was a car show and swap meet in 1981, a tradition that continued on the last Sunday in July every year through 2006. Changing gears to better meet the needs of members, the club now sponsors Cruise Nights every Thursday in downtown Frankfort during the summer, as well as organizing other social, educational, and service events for members. The 1988 car show (pictured above) drew the largest crowd organizers had seen since 1981. (Above, courtesy of Chuck VanderVelde.)

Gardening is a favorite pastime in Frankfort, especially in the historic downtown, where homeowners enjoy re-creating a sense of their houses' histories. Downtown resident and avid gardener Susie Corkery extended her home's charming cottage feel to her yard, where her daughter, Sonnet, had her own pint-size garden tea table (pictured above during a 1992 Frankfort Women's Club garden walk). The Eris Rudman Memorial Garden (right) is also located in the historic district on the Frankfort Founders Center property at Oak and Utah Streets. The Frankfort Garden Club tends to this piece of land, planted in honor of park district organizer Eris Rudman. (Above, photograph by Susie Corkery; right, photograph by Rachel Gilmore.)

For well over 100 years, Frankfort residents have loved their parades. The Frankfort Fall Festival parade, held on the Sunday of Labor Day weekend, is no exception. For decades, people have staked out their territory along the curbs with blankets, chairs, safety cones, and ropes—as early as the night before the parade—and many homeowners along the route host parade parties. This 1990 photograph shows a crowd enjoying the shade and watching the parade pass by at the corner of Walnut and Pacific Streets. (Photograph by Pamela Biesen.)

After the Penn Central Railroad abandoned the former Michigan Central Railroad tracks in the late 1970s, the native prairie began reclaiming its ground. When eco-minded citizens realized what a natural resource lay along the tracks, they formed the Old Plank Road Trail Association to preserve the pieces of prairie and convert the rail line to a walking and biking path. Pictured here are Marian Glunz (front) and Judy Herder (back) clearing brush along the tracks. The trail opened to the public in 1997.

The tavern at 113 Kansas Street has been a local gathering spot for 150 years. Originally built by A.B. Barker, it was home to a drugstore, post office, and farm implement business. Since 1942, it has been a tavern, owned first by Grayce Blalock and for the last decade by Bruce and Pam Patterson. Its big claim to fame, however, was that it was the backdrop for a scene from *Straight Talk*, a 1992 comedy starring James Woods and Dolly Parton. Locals turned out by the dozen to see the action firsthand and maybe even appear in the background. In this photograph, the crew sets up a shot on the tavern porch.

Actor James Woods poses with then curator of the Frankfort Area Historical Society Anne Helms (left), FAHS member Sally Campbell (center), and then village clerk Joanne Mark (right) during a break from filming the 1992 movie *Straight Talk*. Two unidentified men stand behind.

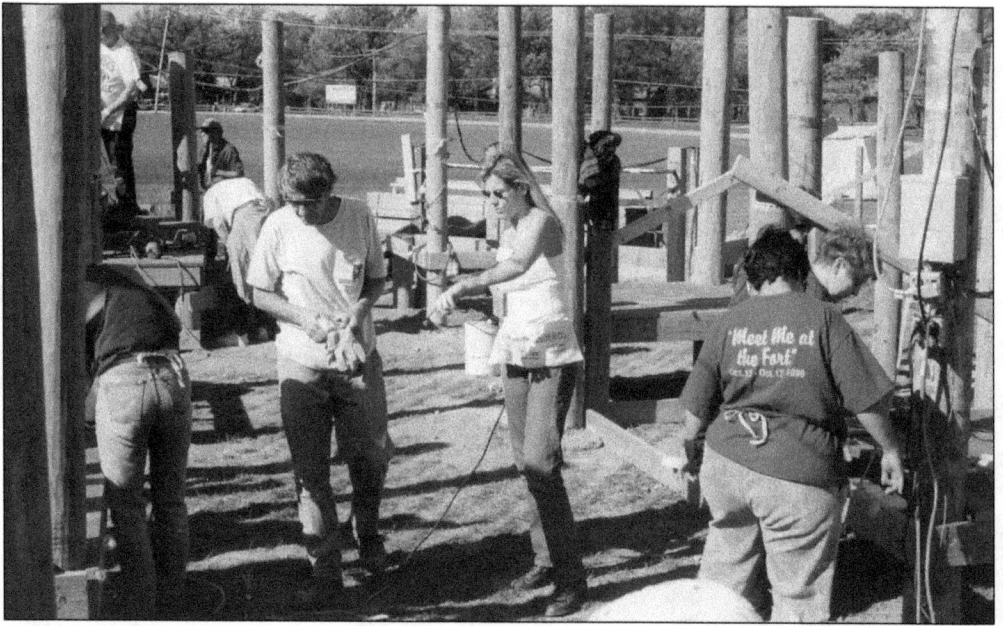

"Meet me at the Fort!" was the slogan for the 1999 community park–building campaign in Frankfort. Designed by Leathers & Associates with resident input (children and adults), this park was born out of sheer determination and hundreds, if not thousands, of volunteer hours. From the planning and fundraising to the on-site building week, the entire community came together to see the fort rise up from its windy patch of prairie. In 2000, Fort Frankfort won the Illinois Association of Park Districts' (IAPD) prestigious Park Facility of the Year award; and its 501C3 organizers, Operation Playground, won the IAPD's Community Service Award. The Governor's Hometown award was also bestowed on Fort Frankfort in 2000. The photograph above shows volunteers discussing a construction issue. The photograph below shows the fort almost completed, with wheelbarrows standing at the ready to move in a literal mountain of mulch to provide the 18-inch-deep play surface. (Both, courtesy of the Frankfort Park District.)

Inspired by a display of Swiss public art they saw in a book, Frankfort residents John and Judy Herder helped fund the Lucy the Library Lactator sculpture for a City of Chicago Public Arts Program street exhibit in 1999. Lucy was painted in a nursery rhyme theme by former Frankfort resident and artist John Santoro (pictured here with Lucy). After Lucy completed her time in Chicago, she was transported to Frankfort and now lives at the Frankfort Public Library. (Courtesy of the Frankfort Public Library District.)

Civil War general William Tecumseh Sherman's horse Sam spent his final years in Frankfort, living the good life on the Sanger farm (now the neighborhood of Connecticut Hills) until his death in 1874. In 2004, the Frankfort Historical Society and the Frankfort Preservation Foundation erected this sculpture on the grounds of the Frankfort Founders Center to honor Sherman and Sam. Pictured behind the sculpture are artist Margi Hafer, FAHS president Judy Herder, and an unidentified woman.

Just the place for your
vacation at

FRANKFORT, ILL.

It's the nicest place I know.

These vintage postcards embody community sentiment about Frankfort. While it is not a vacation destination per se, Frankfort's genuine charm and village-supported family values have made it home to generations of Midwesterners who tell their friends and family, "It's the nicest place I know."

It is very pleasant at

FRANKFORT, ILL.

and the scenery is beautiful.

ABOUT THE ORGANIZATION

The Frankfort Area Historical Society organized in 1972 and has played an active role in preserving, protecting, and promoting Frankfort's history since that time. The museum, once a livery stable owned by Johnson Folkers (one of Frankfort's first residents), is regularly open to the public four days a week and houses an extensive collection of records and memorabilia.

The society's mission statement is as follows: "The society's major function will be to discover and collect any material which may help to establish or illustrate the history of the area. It will collect and preserve printed material, manuscript material and other museum material. The society will disseminate historical information to the public."

Our annual activities include the Holiday Housewalk (first Friday in December); hosting the Lantern Parade during Christkindl (first weekend in December); providing four $1,000 scholarships to two graduating seniors at both Lincoln-Way East and North High Schools; donating memorial books to the Frankfort Public Library; maintaining an extensive photograph library; maintaining an extensive documents library including school records dating back to 1850, local cemetery information, abstracts of old Frankfort homes, maps, plats, and other historical data; preparing displays in the museum which share Frankfort's history; presenting bronze plaques for placement on historical buildings in Frankfort; providing research information to individuals or groups inquiring about families, sites, architecture, or structures; conducting tours for school groups, Scout troops, bus tours, seniors groups, historical societies, or other organizations; and participating in other downtown Frankfort events and activities.

The museum is located at 132 West Kansas Street in Frankfort. Our website is www.frankforthistoricalsociety.org. Our phone number is 815-469-6541.

Visit us at
arcadiapublishing.com

www.ingramcontent.com/pod-product-compliance
Lightning Source LLC
Chambersburg PA
CBHW050623110426
42813CB00007B/1698